A VICTORIAN LADY'S DIARY 1828-1842

ELIZABETH NUTT HARWOOD

C000130251

FOREWORD

The diary of Elizabeth Nutt Harwood is an invaluable historical document. It casts a unique eye on both local issues and events of national importance. Her diary covers a short but highly significant period of five years at the beginning of Queen Victoria's reign and it covers a major period of economic and social development in the Beeston area. The River Trent and Beeston Canal were always busy carrying freight across the region and from 1838 the Midland Counties Railway greatly improved local transport links. Elizabeth had a keen eye for detail. She recorded everything from skating on the Beeston Canal and attending lectures at the National School to the arrival of the first steam train from Nottingham to Derby through Beeston. Some passages relate to travel abroad, emigration to America and the departure of the vicar's son to New Zealand. Weather conditions were a major influence on local life. Fine, sunny weather, was vital for haymaking and harvesting, while icy conditions and heavy rain delayed the barges and cast the boatmen into periods of unemployment. Many labourers and workmen depended on the facilities offered by The Boat Inn for shelter and refreshment. These facilities were considerably improved by the building of the Garden Room.

Page 30.

BAPTISMS solemnized in the Parish of Beeston in the County of Nottingham in the Year 18_18_						
When Baptized.	Child's Christian Name.	Parents Name.		Abode.	Quality, Trade, or Profession.	By whom the Ceremony was performed.
		Christian.	Surname.			
14 Nov. No. 235.	Elizabeth Nutt Daughter of	Richard & Elizabeth	Harwood	Beeston	Boatman	T. Bigsby Vicar.

Fig. 1 Parish register entry, 14 November 1818, for Elizabeth's baptism at Beeston Church

Elizabeth was born on 11th November 1818 at Beeston and was baptised at the parish church on the 14th November. As a young woman she lived at the Boat & Horses Inn, Beeston Meadow, The Rylands. This area included Beeston Canal and the River Trent and was developing into a busy part of Beeston, as barges plied their trade along the waterways. Elizabeth lived with her father Richard and probably helped to run the Inn. She began writing her diary on the 1st January 1838 when she was only 19 years old and continued until December 1842. The diary is in the form of a small notebook, bound in red leather, and marked with the price of 1s 6d. The starting date suggests she received the notebook as a Christmas gift. The entries are written neatly and carefully, generally in pen and ink though some entries are in pencil. After Elizabeth's death, in October 1852, the diary was probably kept in the Harwood family. It was discovered by Mrs Isabel Rowe, a relative of the family, when clearing a relative's home in 1979. Recognizing the diary's importance she generously donated it to Nottinghamshire Archives (County House, Castle Meadow Road, Nottingham) where it is now permanently preserved and available for public consultation. Its reference number is DD 802/1.

Editorial Comment

Elizabeth's diary has been transcribed word for word and most of the spellings, even when incorrect, have been left in their original form. The spellings of their/there is frequently confused. However some spellings and punctuation have been amended to aid the readability of the text. In some instances the correct word has been placed in brackets after her version of the original word. Some punctuation has been added.

ELIZABETH NUTT HARWOOD AND HER FAMILY

Elizabeth was born at the 'Boat & Horses Inn' in Beeston Rylands, a small hamlet south of Beeston, bordering the Canal and the River Trent, on 11 November 1818. She grew to know the area very well, and the local people. Elizabeth's father was Richard Harwood, a yeoman farmer whose family were originally from Radcliffe-on-Trent where they had farmed the land for generations. Her grandfather, also called Richard, was attracted to the Rylands area where land was already enclosed and available for sale. In about 1808 he was able to purchase land by the Canal and establish his own farm in the Rylands. The building of the Canal in 1783 had already brought increased economic activity to the area. Richard's father realised the importance of these local canal schemes and had bought shares in them. He also saw the need for further developments in the Rylands as boatmen and others came into the area to load and unload the many barges. They often needed food and drink and sometimes accommodation. He decided to convert part of the farm buildings into an Inn which he called, very aptly, The Boat and which later became The Boat and Horses. On his death his son, Richard Harwood (Elizabeth's father), inherited the farm – known as Rylands Farm, which comprised two houses, a garden croft, and an orchard with 50 acres of meadow and the Inn. In his farming business Richard became acquainted with local landowners, such as Squire Charlton of Chilwell Hall and businessmen.

Elizabeth's mother was Elizabeth Nutt, the daughter of a prosperous butcher in Lenton whose family eventually acquired a butcher's shop in Beeston. This is probably where Richard became acquainted with her. The couple married at Beeston Church on 2nd October 1817. Elizabeth was born on 11 November 1818, and was the only surviving child. Her mother was delicate and died in 1824 aged 33, when Elizabeth was only 5. It was a family tragedy.

In order for Richard to continue his work as a farmer and the licensee of the Inn, he engaged Mrs Mary Longford, his father's widowed sister, and his sister Betsey Harwood to help him. Mrs Langford (called Aunt Langford) had a son, Tom, living with them and is mentioned in the Diary prior to his early death in 1839.

Elizabeth had close ties with the uncles, aunts and cousins of the Nutt family at Lenton and Beeston. Her father's brother, Robert, had a farm in the Rylands and had a young family at this time. Elizabeth was cared for by her father and the aunts, and as she grew up would be instructed by them in the housewifely arts of cookery and needlework. There was no state education at this time so Elizabeth would have been educated privately at one of the Ladies Academies in the village, probably at the Manor Lodge, founded by Mrs Ward. The Manor Lodge is still to be seen on Middle Street today. Among her particular friends were members of the Barker family. Mr Barker was an agent for the Trent Navigation Company and the family lived at the lock-keeper's cottage. Elizabeth liked to attend Bible Society meetings with Mrs Barker. Elizabeth also seemed to have kept in touch with various neighbours in the area.

Fig. 2 The house (butcher's shop) on Gregory Street, Lenton, where Elizabeth spent her married life with Tom Nutt

Elizabeth married her cousin Tom (Thomas Cornelius Nutt) by licence at Beeston Parish Church on 17 May 1843. Cousin Tom is mentioned many times in the later years of the diary. Tom was a butcher with a shop on Gregory Street in Lenton, which can still to be seen today. After the marriage Elizabeth moved to Lenton and lived with Tom at the shop. Thomas, their first child, was born there in 1845, closely followed by Elizabeth in 1846. However by the 1850s it is evident that Elizabeth's health was failing. By the 1851 census Elizabeth has returned to her old home at the 'Boat Inn' with her little daughter, where she is being cared for by Aunt Betsey and Aunt Langford. She died on 28 October 1852 and was buried in a grave beside her mother in the Churchyard. The grave bears the following inscription:

Sacred
to the memory of
Elizabeth beloved wife of
Thomas Cornelius Nutt
of Lenton in this county,
who after a long and severe affliction
which she bore with patience
and resignation to her divine Maker,
departed this life Oct 28 1852
aged 34 years.

'Farewell
thou busy world where reign,
Short hours of joy and years of pain
Farewell

Fig. 3 Elizabeth's gravestone, Beeston churchyard

(This gravestone can be seen in the churchyard at the back of Wilkinson's shop in the Square.)

In the 1861 Census, Richard Harwood, now 73, is still at the Boat Inn and has both his grandchildren Thomas (16) and Elizabeth (15) living with him. His sister, Alice Harwood is his housekeeper and there are two servants. Thomas is helping on the farm and Elizabeth is still at school. In 1869 Thomas Harwood Nutt had a farm in Beeston. In the 1871 Census the Boat Inn has been taken over by a new licensee. Yet Elizabeth Nutt Harwood's diary remained within the family, carefully preserved and cherished. Today its survival provides us with a wonderful insight into her life and times and that of the world she inhabited.

4

BEESTON
From Village To Town

Beeston was developing from a rural village to an industrial town during the period of the diary. The Enclosure Act of 1806 had released land for sale in the parish and buyers were well aware of the possibilities of building new houses for sale or rent. By 1809 William Fellows had bought land in the north-west of the village to establish his Belle Vue estate. In 1819 Henry Kirkland, a lace manufacturer from Nottingham, had bought land on Moore Gate (off Middle Street) for his lace factory and land on Broadgate for houses for himself and his eldest son. Textiles continued to be of importance in the area. In 1826 William Lowe bought land on the Turnpike (High Road) and erected his silk mill and soon had 200 workers there. By 1844 Thomas Pollard had set up as a Fancy Net and Lace maker. There were still many framework knitters operating in their cottages. All this activity brought workers into Beeston from outlying villages and consequently the population here grew from 1,534 in 1821 to 2,807 in 1844. The arrival of the railway in 1838 ensured Beeston's future development. By 1841, two thirds of the working population here were employed in textile manufacture. In the meantime members of the professional class were taking up residence in Beeston, including solicitors, doctors, auctioneers and schoolmasters. Beeston was a growing and prosperous community.

The Rise of Nonconformity in Beeston

For many years the Anglican church had been at the centre of local life but it had suffered a decline from 1799 -1822. During this time the benefice had been held by the Rev. Thomas Bigsby, who also held the benefice at Arnold. In fact Bigsby chose to live in Arnold and and, as a consequence, his parish at Beeston was neglected. This gave the opportunity for the Nonconformists to come into the area. In 1798 the Methodists from Chilwell were preaching in the streets and had established a meeting house in a barn off Middle Street. In 1803 a small group of Baptists from the area decided to build a small chapel in Nether Street, which in 1806 was enlarged to accommodate the larger congregations. This church still stands but today is used as a day nursery. In 1809 a small group of Wesleyan Methodists were meeting in a house when Henry Kirkland (also a Wesleyan Methodist) came in 1819. He encouraged them to build a chapel on the street opposite his factory in 1825. By this

Fig. 4 The Old Wesleyan Chapel, Chapel Street, Beeston

time the Wesleyans had grown and a new church on the same site was built in 1830. Henry Kirkland, who was also a lay preacher, exerted a great influence there. It was to this Chapel that Elizabeth, Aunt Langford and her son attended. In 1835 Bethel Chapel was built for New Connexion Methodists. In 1838/9 the Baptist chapel had appointed a new young minister, Rev. Francis Smith, who was proving very popular in the village, which explains the reason for Elizabeth and her friends visiting his chapel on some occasions. Later he and some Baptists moved from Nether Street and built a small chapel on Butcher's Lane (Wollaton Road) and they do not appear in the Diary after 1839.

The Revival of the Anglican Church, 1822-1844, in Beeston

In 1822 a new vicar, Rev. Francis Hurt, was appointed to the parish. He later took the name of Rev. Francis Woolley. Owing to years of neglect the vicarage was in a very dilapidated condition so Francis built himself a new Vicarage on Middle Street, which he called Beeston Hall. This was a fine large building to accommodate his large family and servants. The building is now The Cow in Beeston.

In 1835 the National School was founded on Brown Lane (Station Road) to provide education for children belonging to the Church. It was these premises the Vicar used to inaugurate a series of lectures on matters of local interest, which were to prove so interesting to Elizabeth The revival of the church was to encourage the Vicar to urge his parishioners to consider the possibility of building a new church for the parish. This was achieved in 1844.

NOTTINGHAM

In the early nineteenth century Nottingham was a centre of the hosiery and lace trades. The population had grown rapidly as workers moved into the town. As its population grew hundreds of back to back houses were crowded together and many workers lived in poverty. At the same time wealthy manufacturers and businessmen built large, family, houses in up-and-coming areas like the Park.

The borough had a rich commercial life. Crowds gathered in the great, open, Market Place to buy goods that ranged from vegetables to saucepans. The high light of the year was the famous Goose Fair, held in October, when hundreds gathered from near and far to see the side shows and the renowned Bostock & Wombwells Menagerie and other amusements. No wonder Elizabeth enjoyed her visit! The fine Exchange building, which housed the Mayor's apartments and Corporation offices, overlooked the Market Place. Elizabeth's cousins attended a ball at the Exchange on one occasion. The Market Place was also the venue for various open air meetings. John Wesley had preached there in the eighteenth century and in the nineteenth century crowds regularly flocked to the Market Place to listen to political speeches. As a Tory supporter Elizabeth was delighted when her candidate won in 1841.

Nottingham also had a lively social and sporting life. Horse races were held on the Forest, an area of common land just to the north of the town centre. The Castle provided a visual focus for the town though it was then owned by the Duke of Newcastle and held as a ducal residence. Another important feature in Nottingham was the bridge over the Trent. As well as providing a vital crossing point over the river; its long row of arches afforded a fine spectacle for visitors.

LENTON

On its western side Lenton ran along Beeston's boundary. It was an important neighbour. Lenton also included the ruins of the famous Lenton Priory. Lenton was the home of Elizabeth's mother and her uncle's family ran a thriving butchery business on Gregory Street (the house still stands today). Lenton developed rapidly in the late seventeenth and early nineteenth centuries and was fast approaching the boundary with Nottingham on the north and east. Frank Wright, a wealthy industrialist built Lenton Hall on the former Abbey lands. Elizabeth visited the Hall to view its gardens. Today the hall is a University residence. Lenton inhabitants once worshipped at a small church amidst the remains of the priory but by 1842 a new and larger church had been built to serve the expanding population.

THE LECTURES (held at the National School)

1838	January 5	Geology – Mr Greaves
	January 12	Geography – Mr Clark
	January 19	Nutrition – Dr Orton
	February 2	Phrenology – Mr Dorr
	February 16	Phrenology – Mr Dorr
	February 23	Phrenology – Mr Dorr
	March 2	Phrenology – Mr Dorr
	March 9	Phrenology – Mr Dorr
	March 16	Digestion and Intemperance – (Dr Higginbotom)
	March 23	Opticio – Mr Rawson
	March 30	Locomotive Engine
	April 6	Phrenology – Mr Dorr
	April 12	Phrenology – Mr Dorr
	October 17	General Resume – The Vicar
	October 24	Silk and The Silkworm – Mr Robert Felkin
	October 31	Silk and The Silkworm – Mr Robert Felkin
	November 4	Silk and The Silkworm – Mr Robert Felkin
1839	January 2	The Nervous System – Mr Farmer
	January 9	The Steam Engine – Mr Fox
	January 29	Astronomy – Mr Goodacre
	January 30	Astronomy – Mr Goodacre
	February 20	The Improvement of the Mind – Rev. F. Smith
	March 6	The Eye – Dr Win
	March 27	Geography of Palestine – Mr H. Kirkland
	April 3	Geography of Palestine – Mr H. Kirkland
1840	January 28	The Printing Press – Mr Hickling
	February 6	Electricity – (no speaker given)
1841	None mentioned	
1842	May 5	New Zealand Customs etc. – Mr Burns (Maori Chief)
	May 6	New Zealand Customs etc. concluded – Mr Burns (Maori Chief)

Note: Phrenology was the study of character and personality by the shape of a person's head

PRINCIPAL PERSONALITIES mentioned in the Diary

Mr William Barker	- Agent for Trent Navigation Co. and the Lock-keeper
The Vicar	- Rev. F. J. Woolley, Vicarage on Middle Street (now 'The Cow in Beeston')
Mr Smith	- Rev. Francis Smith, Baptist Minister
Mr Freckingham (Frettingham)	- Nursery owner on Nether Street
Mr R. Tebbutt	- Licensee on Turnpike (High Road)
Mr Orton	- Doctor in the village, living in the Manor House
Mr H. Kirkland	- Lace manufacturer (Moore Gate) and lay preacher at Wesleyan chapel, living at the Manor House
Mr Wm. Voce	- Boat builder at Rylands
Mr Robert Felkin	- Lace manufacturer (Villa Street) living in Broadgate
Mr Charlton	- Squire of Chilwell, living at the Hall
Mrs Dickinson	- Licensee of 'Jolly Anglers', Rylands
Mr Wm. Thornhill	- Bespoke tailoring business, house on the Turnpike
Mr Henry Cross	- Blacksmith, living on Middle Street
Mr Dorr	- Phrenologist in Chilwell
Mr Higginbottom	- Surgeon from Nottingham
Mr Rawson	- Optician from Nottingham
Mr Dearden	- Bookseller from Nottingham
Mr Thomson	- Surgeon from Lenton
Mr Hickling	- Printer on the Turnpike
Mr Goodacre	- Head Master of Standard Hill Academy, which was located at College House, Chilwell
Mr Wm. Oldknow	- Lace manufacturer in Nottingham
Mr Frank Wright	- High Sheriff (owner of the Butterley Colliery Co.) living at Lenton Hall
Mr Thomson	- Chemist and Druggist on the Turnpike
Mr Foulds	- Music-seller and Teacher from Nottingham

Jan.ᵗʰ 1ˢᵗ 1838.

Jan.ᵗʰ 1ˢᵗ very fine mild day busy
making pork pyes. Jan.ᵗʰ 2ⁿᵈ very
fine day, I & Aunt Langford went
to and supper to Uncle Robert Nutts
Aunt John Nutt & Mr Weston Mr
Keckingham Miss Cowley Miss Hays
& Mrᶠˢ ᵗᵗ Walker were their, spent
a very merry evening, Jan.ᵗʰ 3ʳᵈ Went
with Miss Ann Barker to invite the
Neighbours to the meeting at Mr Smedleys
took tea with Miss Barker, Jan.ᵗʰ
4ᵗʰ fine day Aunt John & Aunt Robert
Nutt Mrs Weston Miss Cowley Mary
Nutt & Aunt Harwood took tea & supper
with us Mr Weston & Uncle William
came after for them. Jan.ᵗʰ 5ᵗʰ very muggy
all day in the evening I went with Father
& Aunt Langford to here Mr Greaves lecture
on geology which he illustrated by several
several specimens of Rocks & Fossils —

Fig. 5 The first page of Elizabeth's diary

10

January 1838

1st   Very fine and mild day. Busy making pork pyes.

2nd   Very fine day. I & Aunt Langford went to tea and supper to Uncle Robert Nutt's. Aunt John Nutt and Mrs Weston, Mrs Freckingham, Miss Cowley, Miss Day & Mr. Joseph Walker were their (there). Spent a very merry evening.

3rd   Went with Miss Ann Barker to invite the neighbours to the meeting at Mrs Smedley's. Took tea with Miss Barker.

4th   Fine day. Aunt John & Aunt Robert Nutt, Mrs Weston, Miss Cowley, Mary Nutt & Aunt Harwood took tea & supper with us. Mr Weston & Uncle William came after for them.

5th   Very misty all day. In the evening I went with Father & Aunt Langford to hear Mr Greaves lecture on Geology which he illustrated by several specimens of rocks & fossils. Some of them very curious, particularly a part of a mammel's tooth and a part of a deer's horn that had been found a very great depth in the earth and a piece of rock composed entirely of fishes eggs. Was very much interested.

6th   Very misty all day. Aunt Langford & Father went to Nottingham

7th   Dull day. Went to Mr Smith's chappel in the morning. Hannah Hurst was buried in the afternoon at the Church.

8th   Sharp frost morning. Snow in the afternoon.

9th   Sharp frost and snow all day. Uncles John, William and Robert for dinner and tea. Expected Uncle Parr but he did not come.

10th   Frost & snow all day.

11th   Frost & snow all day.

12th   Frost and snow most of the day. In the morning, went with Father and Aunt Langford to here Mr Clark's lecture on Geography. Liked him very much.

13th   Frost with a little snow.

14th   Sharp frost. Went in the morning to Mr Smith's chapple

15th   Sharp frost. Canal frozen over. Some Nottingham gentlemen scated (skated) up in the afternoon.

16th   Continued freezing very sharp.

17th   Sharp frost, little snow in the morning. John Hurst was buried at the Church in the afternoon. In the evening went to the meeting at Mrs Smedley's.

18th   Sharp frost and snow nearly all day.

19th   Very sharp frost, little snow. Went with Aunt Langford to here (hear) Mr Orton's lecture
on   Nutrition, etc. It was very cold indeed.

20th   Very sharp frost. Trent frozen over at Wilford. Aunt Betsy went to Nottingham to stay a week or two. Father and Aunt Langford went with her in the cart.

21st   Sharp frost.

22nd   Thawing very fast. Snow nearly all gone.

23rd   Sharp frost with little snow.

24th   Sharp frost. Small snow most of the day.

25th   Sharp frost with little snow.

26th   Sharp frost with little snow.
27th   Sharp frost.
28th   Sharp frost. Milder in the evening.
29th   Thawing very fast.
30th   Continued thawing.
31st   Sharp frost.

February 1838
1st   Frosty.
2nd   Went to here (hear) Mr. Dorr's lecture on Phranology. Father came home with me. Liked him very much.
3rd   Frost with little snow at night. Aunt Langford went to Nottingham by Clifton. Eliza very ill. Aunt Betsy came home with her. She continues poorly.
4th   Frost. Aunt Langford and Tom in the morning to Clifton. In the afternoon their were a great many gentlemen scated up the Canal.
5th   Weather milder.
6th   Frosty. Aunt Betsy went to Nottingham in the cart. Aunt Langford went with her and came home by Clifton. Eliza a little better. Father went with Uncle Parr to Newark.
7th   Thawing with small rain. Mr Tebbert came and paid Father for the large copper and tub.
8th to11th   Sometimes freasing and sometimes thawing.
12th   Frost. Father went to Leister (Leicester).
13th   Sharp frost. George brought Eliza on the pony to stay few days.
14th   Sharp frost.
15th   Sharp frost. Father and Uncle John, William and Robert went to Uncle Parr's to settle the Trent Navergation shares.
16th   Sharp frost. Went to here Mr Dorr lecture on Phranology. He explained several of the organs of the head and related a many very interesting anectodotes (anecdotes). I liked him very much.
17th   Snow all day. Father and Aunt Langford went to Nottingham in the cart. Aunt Betsy came home with them.
18th   Sharp frost. Went with Aunt Langford to Mr Smith's chapple
19th   Thawing and freezing. Went to the meeting at Mrs Smedley's.
20th   Thawing and freezing.
21st   Thawing and freezing.
22nd   Frost.
23rd   Snow most of the day. Went with Aunt Langford to here (hear) Mr Dorr lecture on Phrenology. He produced the explanation of the differant organs of the head. Was very interested. Came home with Mr and Mrs Barker.
24th   Thawing very fast. Rain and sleet most of the day.
25th   Sleet in the morning, fine in the afternoon.
26th   Snow and rain.

27th   Snow and rain, and sleet all day.
28th   Dull with little rain.

March 1838

1st   Dull with little rain.
2nd   The weather much milder. Went in the evening with Aunt Langford to hear Mr Dorr give another lecture on Phranology. There was a very large congregation. Was very interested.
3rd   Fine day. A flood on the Trent.
4th   Rain most of the day.
5th   Fine day.
6th   Fine day.
7th   Stormy all day.
8th   Fine day. Aunt Langford and Aunt Betsy and Eliza went to Nottingham. Eliza went to Clifton.
9th   Fine day. Went with Aunt Langford to here Mr Dorr give another lecture on that very interesting science Phrenology. He finished explaining the organs of the head. Expect him giving two or three more lectures.
10th   Fine day. Father and Aunt Langford went to Nottingham. Eliza came back.
8th-10th Eliza having recovered from her recent illness goes to Clifton for a job interview but returns, obviously unsuccessful.
11th   Rather dull. Went to chaple in the afternoon. Mr Edwards preached.
12th   Fine day. Aunt Langford and Eliza went to Sandacre (Sandiacre).
13th   Rather dull.
14th   Very rough wind.
15th   I and Aunt Langford went with Eliza to Sandacre to live at Mr Gordon's.
16th   Rather dull. Aunt Langford and Father went to here Mr Higerbotam lecture on digestion and intemperence. The room very full. Was much interested.
17th   Rather dull.
18th   Fine day. Went to Mr. Smith's chaple in the evening with Aunt Langford.
19th   Very fine day.
20th   Very rough wind with showers.
21st   Very rough wind with showers. Went in the evening to the meeting at Richardsons.
22nd   Windy with showers.
23rd   Snow in the morning. In the evening to here Mr Rowson's lecture on Optics. Was much interested with his optical instruments and explanation of the eye. The room was very full. Came home with my Father.
24th   Fine day. Little rain in the evening.
25th   Fine day.
26th   Gloomy.
27th   Very fine day. Busy gardening.

28th   Very fine day.

29th   Fine day.

30th   Fine day. Father and I went in the evening to here Mr Rowan lecture on local motive (locomotive) engins and the general construction of Railways – which he explained cleverly (in my weak oppinion of such matters). The room was very crowded and warm.

31st   Rather dull all day.

April 1838

1st   Fine day but very cold.

2nd   Dull day with little wind.

3rd   Fine in morning. Clowdy in afternoon. Father and I walked to Nottingham and from their to Snenton (Sneinton) with Aunt Alice and Miss Crawshaw to see Earl Manvass (Manvers) lay the corner stone of the new church. Their were thought to be fifteen thousand persons preasent and about five hundred of the National and Blue Coat School Boys & Girls and several clergymen with the Earl walked in procession but they were obliged to retire without concluding the whole of the Ceremony. There was such a disgraceful confusion all the time and such an uncommon rush of the people to see the stone.

4th   Fine day. Busy making poark pyes. Went in the evening to the meeting at Richardsons.

5th   Stormy.

6th   Dull all day. I and Aunt Langford went to here Mr Dorr lecture on Phranology. Was much interested. Expect him concluding the lectures for this season next Thursday evening.

7th   Showery with very high wind all day.

8th   Dull and stormy.

9th   Cold most of the week.

10th   Cold most of the week.

11th   Cold most of the week.

12th   Fine day. Aunt Langford and I went to here Mr Dorr conclude his lectures on Phranology and the last for this season. It was very interesting. He brought with him the bust of Greenacre, the London Murderer. He explained the organs of his head, and gave a short account of his life, which was certainly very awful. He related some interesting anecdotes.
        The Rev. J. Wolley read a paper on the different subjects that had been lectured on and thanked the lecturer and the people for their attendance. Mr Dorr concluded the meeting.

13th   Fine day. Cousin Mary Nutt and Miss Hopkin came over in the afternoon. This is Good Friday.

14th   Very rough day.

15th   Showers with rough wind all day.

16th   Very cold with little snow.

17th   Very cold with snow storms.

18th   Cold with wind and little snow.

July 1838

4th   My poor Journal. I have quite forgotton you, but I have not a great deal of news to write. Our beloved Queen Victoria was crowned on the 28th June, there was a great deal of rejoiceing all over the country, except at poor Beeston Meadow. At Nottingham there was a public breakfast at the Excange (Exchange) rooms at 9 o'clock or half past. The children of the vaireous sunday schools in the town met in the Market Place and then walked in procession through the streets. In the afternoon the soulgers (soldiers) met in the market place and fired their guns in honour of the day. At night there was fireworks in the market place which was very grand, though I did not see them.

8th   Fine day. This is Beeston Feast. Mr and Mrs Creasey and Mr/Mrs Harvey came to tea. We had a good deal of company after tea.

9th   Very fine day. Miss Hannah Barker and I went a walk after tea.

10th   Fine day. Dull in the evening. Miss Hannah Barker and I went after tea to here Mr Smith address the sunday school scolars from the differant chaples in Beeston at the Methedost (Methodist) Chaple which he did in a very impressive manner.

11th   Dull day. Rain in the afternoon. I went to Beeston this morning to see for Father. He is waning a bit. He went on Monday night and is not come back yet. I found him in bed at Mr Teberts. He came home about 7 o'clock.

12th   Rather dull.

13th   Dull day. Began to mow the meadow.

Fig. 6 The Exchange, Nottingham, 1845

14th   Dull in the morning, rain all afternoon. Went with Miss Hannah Barker to Nottingham

15th   Showery all day. Father very porley (poorly)

16th   Showery all day. Father very porley.

17th   Fine day. Had 9 men haymaking.

18th   Fine day. Had 13 men haymaking. It is Aunt Betsy's birthday. Got 9 loads of hay home.

19th   Fine day. Had 13 men haymaking. Got 16 loads home.

20th   Fine day. Finished getting the hay all but about one load.

21st   Fine day. Finished the hay. Had 36 loads out of the Beeston Meadow and 10 out of the Home Close. Got it all well.

22nd   Showery.

23rd   Rather dull with little wind.

24th   Fine day. Mrs Shelton and Aunt Alice came. They with Aunt Langford and I went to Mr Smith's chaple in the evening.

25th   Rather dull. Mrs Shelton and Aunt Alice went home after tea.

26th   Cold.

27th   Cold for the time of the year.

28th   Cold for the time of the year.

29th   Cloudy and very cold. Went to Mr Smith's chapel in the evening.

30th   Stormy. Went to spend afternoon with cousin Jane Nutt at Uncle Robert Nutt's. She is keeping house for him whilst Aunt is gone to Tutbury.

31st   Dull day. Fine in the evening. I took a walk with Miss Hannah Barker and Miss Powell.

August 1838

1st   Fine day.

2nd   Cloudy most of day. Aunt Langford and I took a walk to Barton after tea.

3rd   Dull day.

4th   Dull with little rain in the morning. Father took cart to Nottingham to be painted.

5th   Cloudy. Aunt Langford and I went to Mr Smith's chaple in the afternoon. There were 7 baptised.

6th   Cloudy with rough wind.

7th   Cloudy in the morning, fine in afternoon.

8th   Fine day. Aunt Langford and Aunt Betsy went to Nottingham

9th   Dull day with little rain in morning. Aunt Langford and Aunt Betsy went this morning by the 11 o'clock coach to Ashby to stay a week or two. I feel very much lost indeed. Shall be very glad when they get home again.

10th   Very dull and damp.

11th   Fine day. Mr Joseph Taylor came and gave orders for a party on Monday next.

12th   Fine day. Uncle Parr walked over in afternoon. Expect Aunt Alice tomorrow to assist with party.

13th   Fine day this morning. Father laid the first block of the Railway after which all the contractors, the engeneers and several of there freinds dined hear on the grass plot.

They spent a very merry day – there were about 34 of them. Miss Britemore cooked for us and Aunt Alice came with father in the cart to assist us.

14th   Fine day. Busy getting the things away after the party. Received a letter from my aunts at Ashby. Aunt Alice went home after tea. Miss Ann Barker caled (called) in the evening.

15th   Fine day.

16th   Fine day.

17th   Fine day. I wrote a note to send tomorrow to my Aunts at Ashby.

18th   Fine day. Father went to Nottingham and brought the cart home. It has been painted and looks much better. The Clifton Band came over in evening and played in the Dining Room.

19th   Cloudy most of the day with showers.

20th   Fine day.

21st   High wind with flying showers.

22nd   Very rough wind. Have had several and very heavy showers of Thunder and rain.

23rd   Rain most of the day. My Aunt Langford and Aunt Betsy came home from Ashby.

24th   Rain most of the day.

25th   Dull with showers of rain. Father went to Nottingham Aunt Langford & I went to Beeston to look at some things that have been left in one of our houses for rent.

26th   Fine day. Went to Bethall Chaple in the morning.

27th   Fine day. Went to library in the evening.

28th   Fine day – dull in the afternoon. Very awful thunder and lightening at night till about 12 o'clock.

29th   Fine day. Went to chaple at night.

30th   Fine day. Took tea at Mr Barker's.

31st   Fine day.

September 1838

1st   Fine day. Aunt Langford and I went to Nottingham. Father got the corn.

2nd   Fine day.

3rd   Fine day.

4th   Fine day. Took a walk in the evening with Miss Hannah Barker.

5th   Several heavy showers during the day.

6th   Dull with little rain.

7th   Dull and damp with little rain. Miss Hannah Barker slept here.

8th   Fine day. Aunt Langford went to Nottingham.

9th   Fine day. Went to chaple in the morning.

10th   Fine day.

11th   Fine day. Miss Harriatt Barker was married to day to Mr William Smedley. I went to church with them. Miss Ann Barker was bridesmaid, Mr Barker, bridesman. Mr T. Smedley, Miss Hannah & Fanny Barker & myself went to church with them. I spent the day with them.

12th	Fine day. Aunt Langford went to tea to Mr Barker's. Cousin Mary Nutt came over to stay a few days with us.
13th	Fine day. Mr & Mrs Smedley, Miss Hannah and Mary Ann Barker, Cousin Mary & myself went to Clifton and enjoyed ourselves very much.
14th	Fine day.
15th	Fine day. Father, Aunt Langford and Mary Nutt went to Nottingham.
16th	Fine day. The Northern Lights were very bright & grand at night.
17th	Fine day.
18th	Fine day. Father took the cart to Nottingham for Aunt Parr. She is come to stay a few days with us.
19th	Fine day. Cousin Mary and I went to tea to Aunt Nutt's at Beeston.
20th	Fine day. Cousin Mary went home. I shall feel very much lost without the merry girl.
21st	Fine day.
22nd	Fine day. Father took the cart to Nottingham. Aunt Parr went home. I went with them.
23rd	Fine in the morning. I went to Mr Smith's chaple in the afternoon. Rain at night.
24th	Rain all day and night.
25th	Dull all day.
26th	Dull all day.
27th	Dull all day. Mr Crashaw and Uncle Parr came a-fishing.
28th	Fine day.
29th	Fine day. Father and Aunt Langford went to Nottingham in the cart. Cousin Eliza is come from Linby to stay a few days with us.
30th	Fine day. Cousin Ann Bailey came over from Lenton.

October 1838

1st	Fine day. Eliza took a walk to Clifton.
2nd	Fine day. This is Goose Fair. Cousin Eliza & I went to Mr. Langford's at Nottingham to stay all night.
3rd	Very fine day. Cousin Eliza and I came home from the Fair having enjoyed ourselves very much.
4th	Fine day.
5th	Fine day. Father went to Nottingham for the chees(e).
6th	Fine day. Father, Aunt Langford and Aunt Betsy, Eliza and Tom went to Nottingham in the cart. Cousin Eliza went home.
7th	Fine day. I went to chapel in the morning.
8th	Dull all day. I went to the Library in the evening. Came home with Miss Hannah Barker.
9th	Cloudy and cold.
10th	Clear and cold. Father is gone to the races.
11th	Clear and v. cold. Father is gone to the races in the cart.
12th	Clear and very cold indeed. There was a snowstorm at Nottingham. Father is gone to the races.

13th	Very cold.
14th	Cold with rain most of the day.
15th	Stormy.
16th	Very damp with showers.
17th	Dull and rather cold. The lectur(e)s for the (*no entry*) commensed this evening. Father and I went. They are not conducted the same as they were last winter. Every one that chouse went to them last year but them that go this have to pay but they that are subscribers to the library go free and they that are not pay 6d per month or take a 2/6d ticket for the winter. Father is a subscriber & I have got a ticket for the winter. The Rev'nd J. Wolley gave the first lecture. He began by showing the use of the knowledge of (*no entry*) and took a general view of all the subjects that had been lectured on last winter. He read some extracts from differant authors on Natural History, Astronomy, Geology, etc. and I think I never heard a more interesting lecture. The meeting was a very respectable one.
18th	Very rough wind.
19th	Fine day. Cousin Ann Bailey came to stay a few days.
20th	Dull and cold.
21st	Fine day. I went to the Chapel in the morning & night. Uncle John came over. Cousin Ann Bailey went home.
22nd	Rather dull.
24th	Dull day. Tom and I went in the evening to hear Mr Felkin lecture on the silkworm. The production of silk from the East and introduction into England on the silk trade generally. He traced silk from 3000 years ago till the preasant time. He has a remarkable memory of the dates, etc. It was very interesting. Father came home with us.
25th	Dull day and cold.
26th	Fine day though cold.
27th	Rain all day. Father & Aunt Langford went to Nottingham in the cart and hired Bessy Preston of Edwalton.
28th	Fine day. I went to chaple in the morning. Uncle John came over in the afternoon.
29th	Stormy.
30th	Fine day, Aunt Langford and I went to a tea meeting at Bethal Chaple I went up with Miss Mary Barker, Mrs Barker, Miss Hannah Turney and Ann Topley came home with us.
31st	Fine day. I went in he evening with Mrs & Miss Mary Barker to here Mr Felkin give another lecture on the silkworm and silk traid. Was much interested. Uncle Robert Nutt received a letter from Aunt Nutt of Tutbury with the sudden news that poor Uncle John was dead. He died on Tuesday, 30th, of inflammation on the chest. He was not ill a week.

November 1838

1st	Cold & stormy. We have got the bricklayers haultering (altering) the stable doors.

2nd   Rough, cold & stormy.

3rd   Rain most of the day.

4th   Dull with rain all morning. Fine in the afternoon. Dull and cold all week. I did not go to the lecture on Wednesday. Mr Felkin concluded his lectures on the Silk Trade, etc.

10th   Dull day. Father and Aunt Langford went to Nottingham in the cart. It is my birthday.

11th   Fine day. I went to chaple in the morning and evening.

12th   Dull day. I began to work myself a pair of shoes.

13th   Cold with sharp frost.

14th to 20th Very sharp frost & uncommonly misty. Several carts stopt. I did not go to the lecture.

21st   Mostly cold and damp. Very cold. I went to here Mr John Dearden lecture at Beeston – was much interested. I came home with Mrs and Miss Mary and Miss Hannah Barker.

22nd   Rain all day.

23rd   Fine day, though very cold. Father went with Mr Smith and Mr Saxton to the Trent Lock.

24th   Little snow in the morning; fine in the afternoon. Father went to Nottingham. James went home.

25th   Very sharp frost. Cold and fine all day. In the afternoon I went to Church with Miss Mary Barker, Mr Woolley preached. Uncle John came over.

26th   Sharp frost.

27th   Sharp frost. Father hired a man.

28th   Rain and high wind all day. I did not go to the lecture.

Fig. 7 The Reverend J.F.T. Woolley, vicar of Beeston 1822 - 1854

29th   Stormy. James came back.

30th   Dull day.

December 1838

1st   Fine day. Rain in the morning. Father and Aunt Langford went to Nottingham in the cart. Our Old Man and Maid left and the new ones came.

2nd   Fine day. I went to chaple in the morning.

5th   Fine Day. Miss Mary Barker and I went to hear Mr Greaves' lecture.

8th   I went to Nottingham in the cart with Father and Mrs & Miss Hannah Barker.

9th   Sharp frost. I went to chapel in the morning.

10th   Cold and misty.

11th   Dull and misty.

12th   Dull and misty. Miss Mary Barker and I went to here Mr Dorr lecture on that very interesting science Phrenology. He gave his introduction lecture before. I did not here it. He explained 4 of the organs beginning with Individuality, then Form, Size & Colouring. He related some interesting anecdotes.

13th   Very misty. Poor Mr Voce died last night about ½ past 10 o'clock

14th   Very damp and misty.

15th   Very misty. Father went to Nottingham in the cart.

16th   Very misty and cold all day.

17th   Very damp and misty. Mr Voce was buried. Father went to the funiral.

18th   Fine day.

19th   Damp day. Aunt Robert Harwood had a daughter about 8 o'clock at night.

20th   Damp and misty.

21st   Damp and misty. I went to Beeston in the afternoon with Miss Mary Barker.

22nd   Damp and misty. Father & Aunt Langford, Miss Mary and Hannah Barker went to Nottingham in the cart.

23rd   Very damp. I went to Chaple in the evening to here Mr Voce's Funeral Sermon. He has bequeathed £200 to the Bethal Chaple and £200 to the General Baptist Chaple to build a house for the Minister at each place. John Mather died at T. Pailthorp's about 10 o'clock at night.

24th   Damp and misty with little rain.

25th   Fine and frosty. This is Christmas Day. We have not had much company.

26th   Frosty in the morning. Rain in the afternoon. Our new man ran away.

27th   Fine day though cold.

28th   Fine day. I went to Beeston in the afternoon. There was a Ball at Beeston in the evening.

29th   Dull and very damp and dirty.

30th   Damp day. Aunt Langford & I went to Chapel in the morning. Mr Kirkland preached a very appropriate Sermon for the last Sunday in the year. Uncle John came over.

31st   Fine day. The year came in with a fine day, and has gone out the same.

January 1839

1st   Changeable though fine for the time of the year. How many there are that have seen the first day of the year before the close will be lade (laid) in their silent grave. Aunt Langford went to a tea meeting at the Bethal Chaple.

2nd   Dull most of the (day). Father and I went in the evening to here Mr Farmer lecture on the Nerves (nervous) Sistam (System). He told us about the nerves of the eyes, nose, mouth, etc. The room was not full.

3rd   Rough wind. I went to tea to Mrs Barker's. Miss Barker is a little better. There was a Ball at Beeston at Mr Tibberts.

4th   Fine day though cold in the evening.

5th   Fine and frosty morning. Aunt Langford and I walked to Nottingham. Father did not go.

6th   Snow in the morning though fine. Rain and wind at night. Mr and Mrs Ward came over and staid (stayed) all night.

| 7th | Rough wind indeed. It blew some dreadfull gusts of wind about 7 o'clock. Our taproom chimbney caught fire. It had been burning some time before we found it out. We had a large fire in the grate at the time. We sleaked it out directly but it did not put it out in the chimbney.
| | Father got some blankets wet and pushed them up as far as he could and let them be up till after dinner. When he took them down it began to burn again. They put the large ladder up and a boatman poured some water down it which put the fire out. We were very glad. We were so much afraid of the stacks and stables, etc. catching fire. It blew the straw stack and a waggin (wagon) load of straw over. We have heard of a great deal of damage been done by the wind. Tom was very frightened indeed.
| 8th | Cold morning. The ground was covered with snow. Some heavy storms of wind and snow in the afternoon.
| 9th | Thawed & rained a little in the night & then frose (froze). It made the ground very slippery. Father, Miss Mary Barker and I went to here Mr Fox lecture on the energy of steam, stationnary and locomotive steam engines. He had some large drawings of engines, etc. Was much interested.
| 10th | Frost in the morning. Thawing in the evening.
| 11th | Damp all day.
| 12th | Fine day. Father and Mrs & Miss Hannah Barker and I went to Nottingham the cart.
| 13th | Fine for the time of the year. I went to chaple in the morning.
| 14th | Frost in the morning. Cold and showery in the afternoon. We killed a pig.
| 15th | Rain in the morning with little snow.
| 16th | Very sharp frost. Making poark pies.
| 17th | Very sharp frost. Canal frozen over in the morning.
| 18th | Sharp frost all day. Mild at night
| 19th | Rain in the morning; fine in the afternoon.
| 20th | Little frost in the morning. Rain in the evening. Uncle Robert's little girl Christened Eliza at the church.
| 21st | Rain all morning. Fine in the afternoon.
| 22nd | Fine day. I went to Lenton to spend a day or two.
| 23rd | Fine day though cold and rather frosty. I went to Nottingham with Cousin Mary Nut(t). Cousin Jane and Tom went to a Ball last night at the Exchange.
| 24th | Fine day with little frost. I have got very sore eyes.
| 25th | Fine and cold day. Cousin Mary and I went to see Mrs Harvey. She has got a son.
| 26th | Little snow. I came home having enjoyed myself very much with Aunt Langford.
| 27th | Cold with little snow.
| 28th | Sharp frost. Little snow in the evening. Msrs Weston and Miss Cowley to tea. Tom is very poorly.
| 29th | Very cold with storms and snow & rain. Father and I went to hear Mr Goodacre lecture on Astronomy. He told us about (the) earth, moon, the cause of eclipses, etc. He is to conclude the subject tomorrow night.

30th Sharp frost. Father and I went to here Mr Goodacre conclude his very interesting lectures. He had a very beautiful orrery (*an astronomical instrument*) & a great many diagrams. He told us about the planets, the starry heavens (and) expansive Universe, etc. They have been the most interesting lectures I ever heard. He delivered them in one of the National Schoolrooms. It was well filled both evenings. Tom is very poorly.

31st Very cold with storms of snow.

February 1839

1st Sharp frost. Ground covered with snow, 3 or 5 inches thick. Canal frozen – very broken up in the afternoon.

2nd Began to thaw about dinnertime.

3rd Continuous thawing. Aunt Langford and I went to chaple in the morning. I forgot to write yesterday that Eliza came from Linby. She has left her place through illhealth. Tom continues very poorley.

4th to 16th Very changeable. I think Eliza a little better, but Tom is much worse than he was.

17th Fine cold day. Aunt Alice came over to see Tom. Went home with Uncle John.

18th Cold with little snow. Eliza a little better. Tom about the same.

19th Very cold with rimey frost. Tom no better.

20th Fine cold day. Aunt & I went to here Mr Smith lecture on the Improvement of the Mind. It was a very instructive lecture.

21st Very cold and fine. Tom no better.

22nd Cold with rain in the afternoon.

23rd Fine day. Mr Orten and Mr Thompson came to see Tom. He is very poorly indeed.

24th Fine day. Eliza and I went to chapel in the morning. Tom has had a rather better night, but has been very sick and ill all day.

25th Cold with showers. Tom very sick and ill. He walked down the garden with my Aunt Langford.

26th Fine day. Tom is not any better. He came downstairs in the morning, but went to bed again before dinner.

27th Cold with little rain at night. Poor Tom is no better. Very sick and in bed all day. Aunt Langford and I went at night for some medicine for him.

28th Fine day. Poor Tom about the same. It is fiveteen years to day since my dear Mother died.

March 1839

1st Fine in the morning, cold at night. Poor Tom is not any better.

2nd Rain in the morning. Fine in the afternoon. Eliza went to Nottingham. Tom seems much better today.

3rd Fine day though cold. Poor Tom is worse today. Uncle Parr came over the afternoon.

4th Fine drying day. Poor Tom about the same. Mr Tomson and Mr Orton met here.

5th Fine cold day. Poor Tom is no better to day.

6th	Cold day with storms and snow. Poor Tom is very bad. Has had a very bad night. I sat with him till 2 o'clock last night. Father and I went to here Dr William's lecture on the eye. Was much interested.
7th	Snow all day and very cold. Father is gone to March Fair. Poor Tom is very bad. He eats scarcely anything at all. He is uncommonly weak and exhausted.
8th	Very cold. The ground covered with snow. Poor Tom is very bad. He was a very great deal worse today. About 2 o'clock we thought the Dear Boy would have died. He has the fainting fits so very bad when he has been to sleep. I sat up with him till (until) towards morning when Aunt Betsy got up and I went to bed.
9th	Sharp frost. Poor Tom seems about the same. John came in the morning. Father took the cart to Nottingham. Aunt Alice and Miss Thorpe came back with him. Eliza sat up with Tom last night.
10th	Sharp frost in the morning. Mr and Mrs Langford came to dinner. George, John and Uncle John came over in the afternoon. Mr Langford took the cart. Mrs Langford & Aunt Alice and Miss Thorp went home in it. James fetched it back. Tom continues to get weaker every day. He appeared brisker this afternoon with seeing his Uncles and Aunts, etc. around him. I sat up with him last night till 4 o'clcok.
11th	Cold drying day. Tom is about the same. Has been very sick most of the night. Aunt Betsy sat up with him. Mr Thomson and Mr Orton came this morning. Eliza and I went to Beeston after tea for some things kind Aunt Alice has sent poor Tom.
12th	Fine day. Poor Tom has had a very bad night. I sat up with him. He seems a little brisker this afternoon. George came over. Mr Hurt brought him a chicking (chicken).
13th	Rain most of the day. Poor dear Tom has had another and restless sick night and Aunt Betsy sat up with him. He appears much worse today. he was very much exhausted to day with some medicine he had had this morning. Aunt Langford has got a fad face and is very poorly. She had scarcely had any sleep for 2 or 3 weeks with always being with poor Tom. He does not like her to leave him at all.
14th	Rain most of the day. Mr Abbot called. Dear Tom is worse today. He has had a very bad night. I sat up with him. He is so very sick. He has not eat anything today except two oisters. he takes a little brandy and water or barley water and such things. Sometimes he appears to be sinking fast. Mrs Barker called in the afternoon.
15th	Rain in the morning. Rather finer in the afternoon. It is with deep sorrow I have tow rite the death of my dear Cousin Tom. He died about 12 o'clock today. Dear Boy, There is an end of his sufferings which have been very seveare. We hope to meit him again in a better world where the weary are at rest. My Aunt Langford was with him when he died. He had a very restless last night. My Aunt Betsy sat up with him. There have mostly been one of us sat with him at night as well as my Aunt Langford who seldom left him. He would have been 18 years of age if he had lived till 3rd April. Father went to Nottingham in the afternoon.

Tis ever thus, Tis ever thus
   With all things here below:
   The noblest, lovelyest, Fairest
   Are always first to go.
   The Bird that sings, sings he sweetist,
   The Pine that crowns the rock,
   The glory of the Garden,
   And the flower of the flock.

16th   Rain in the morning, finer in the afternoon. Father, Aunt Langford, Miss Hannah Barker
       and I went to Nottingham in the cart to provide for the funeral of my dear Cousin Tom.
       Had tea at Mr Langford's. Miss Hannah Barker is very poorley again.
17th   Rain most of the day. George and John came over. Eliza went to chaple at night.
18th   Rain most of the day. Miss Morley helping us to make mourning.
19th   Fine day. Father and I went to Nottingham in the afternoon in the cart to fetch some
       things for dear Tom's funeral.
20th   Rain most of the day. We have this day consined (consigned) to the grave the remains
       of my dear Cousin Tom Langford. We buried him in the churchyard at Beeston. My Aunt
       Alice and Uncle John, George & John & Uncle William came and Mrs Barker and Mrs
       Wootton. Aunt Alice staid at home and we all went to pay the last Tribute of respect to
       poor Tom. The bairers (bearers) were Richard Hewitt, Tom Smedley, Tom Butler,
       George Godlin, Tom Hewitt and James Wilson. We took him in the cart up the fields.

Fig. 8 Beeston Parish Church circa 1840

21st   Fine day. Aunt Langford went to tea to Mr Barker's.

22nd   Fine in the morning, showery in the afternoon. Aunt Langford and I went to Beeston after tea.

23rd   Stormy. Father went to Nottingham

24th   Fine day. Aunt Langford, Eliza and I went to chaple in the morning. Eliza and I went to Church in the afternoon and saw poor Tom's grassey bed.

25th   Stormy. Eliza went to Clifton.

26th   Very fine day. I have been gardening to day. I felt very lost with not having Tommy to help me.

27th   Rain most of the morning. Fine in the afternoon. The hedge at the top of the Croft cut.

28th   Stormy. Father bought a cow at Nottingham I received a letter from Miss Hannah.

29th   Fine cold day. This Good Friday we had a good deal of company. Some Nottingham gentleman (gentlemen) came between 12 and 1 o'clock to dinner and some had tea.

30th   Very cold day. Aunt Langford went to Nottingham. Father took some bills to the Railway Office at Lenton.

31st   Cold day. Aunt Langford and I went to chaple morning & night.

April 1839

1st   Very cold day. Eliza came from Clifton. We killed two of the little pigs.

3rd   Very cold drying day. Aunt Langford and I went at night to here Mr Kirkland lecture on the Geography of Palestine. (He gave one on the same subject last week but I did not go.) It was very instructive and interesting.

4th   Very cold drying day.

5th   Very cold with snow all morning and rain most of the afternoon. George came over in the evening.

6th   Very cold fine day. Eliza went to Clifton.

7th   Canal frozen over in the morning. Very fine in the afternoon. Mr and Mrs George Harvey, Mr and Mrs G. Harvey and Aunt Alice came in the afternoon. Mr Kirkland preached my dear Cousin Tom's funeral sermon. I was very much disappointed; I would not go.

8th   Fine cold day. Eliza went to live at Mr Adams at Bramcott (Bramcote). Aunt Langford, Miss Cowley and myself walked with her after tea. Aunt Alice went home earlay in the morning.

9th   Very cold fine day.

10th   Fine day. Aunt Langford and Ann went to Nottingham. Miss Mary and Fanny Barker, Miss Prowett and I went to Beeston after tea. There was not any lecture.

11th   Cold dry day. Mr Smith & Mr Suton from Nottingham came to dinner. Father went to Trent Lock with them. Miss Hopkin and Cousin Mary Nutt came in the afternoon.

12th   Fine and cold dry day.

13th   Very fine dry day.

14th   Dry day. Ann is poorly.

15th   Fine dry day.

16th   Fine dry day. Father took the cart to Nottingham for Aunt Parr and Mrs Spray and took them back after tea. We have heard that Mrs Hadam where Eliza lives at is dead.

17th   Fine cold day. Rain in the afternoon. We expected Mr Hickling to lecture tonight, but he is very ill.

18th   Cold day, little rain at night. Aunt Langford and I went to the Meeting at Richardsons.

19th   Fine and cold dry day. Father and Aunt Langford went to Nottingham.

21st   Cold dry day. Aunt Langford and I went in the morning to chaple.

22nd   Fine dry day. The steam engine on the railway came up to day. We saw it pass.

23rd   Dull day with little rain. A steam engine(e)with one of the carriages full of gentlemen came up to day and past about ½ past 2 o'clock. Father, Aunt Langford and I went to look at it. It moved majestickly and beautifully along. There was a very great many peopal (people) to see them pass. It is a very handsom(e) engine.

25th   Very fine day. Some Nottingham gentlemen called in the morning and went to Trent Lock and back this way.

26th   Very fine day. Aunt Langford and I went in the evening to Bramcott to see Eliza.

27th   Fine day. Father and Aunt Langford went to Nottingham.

28th   Very fine day.

29th   Fine day. Miss Mary Barker and I walked to Beeston in afternoon.

30th   Find warm day. Been very busy sweeping the grass plot and cleaning the gardin up.

31st   Fine day.

May 1839

1st   Fine day. Miss Cowley walked down in the evening.

2nd   Very fine day.

3rd   Dull in the morning; fine in afternoon.

5th   Fine warm day. Aunt Langford went to Lenton in the morning and I went to chaple.

6th   Fine day.

7th   Fine day. Aunt Langford and I went to Nottingham. Uncle Parr has got the Gout very bad. The Yeoman Cavalry are up exercising for eight days. We saw them come into the Market Place to be dismissed.

8th   Very fine day.

9th   Dull in the morning; rain in the afternoon and very cold.

10th   Cold with little rain.

11th   Cold day.

12th   Very cold in the morning. Cousin Jane Nutt and Mr Moore came to dinner and tea.

13th   Very cold and rather stormy.

14th   Very cold in the afternoon. There was a snowstorm. It is rather uncommon to have snow in May. It was 2 or 3 inches thick and I snowbald (snowballed) the servants. The flowers looked very beautiful peeping from under the snow.

15th   Sharp frost last night. The snow lay on the ground till 8 o'clock. Very cold most of the day though fine.

16th   Very cold. A heavy storm of hale (hail) about noon. Mr & Mrs Harvey came.

17th   Fine day. Aunt Langford and I walked to Bramcott in the evening.

18th   Fine day. Dull in the evening; rain at night. Aunt Langford and Father went to Nottingham.

19th   Dull warm day. This is Whit Sunday.

20th   Fine warm day. I went to Lenton to stay a few days. Uncles had a good deal of Company.

21st   Fine warm day.

22nd   Stormy in the morning. Fine afterwards. Cousin Jane, Mary and I went to Nottingham in the evening. Father came to Lenton.

23rd   Very warm, dusty day. Cousin Mary and I went to Nottm. Forrest to see the 5th Dragoons, the Riflemen, Rocket Brigade and Artillery that are quartered in Nottingham (it is the Queen's Birthday tomorrow and they are keeping it today). They first met in the Market Place and fired a feu-de-joie, then went to the Forrist (Forest) and went through several manouvres and we were too late to see them come back to the Market Place and drank the Queen's health & gave 3 hartey cheers, then retired. They looked very beautiful. There are more soulgers (soldiers) in Nottingham than have been for a very long time. The country is in such aggated (agitated) state with the Chartists. They had a large meeting on the Forrist yesterday.

24th   Dull in the morning. Very fine in the afternoon. Cousin Mary and I went to Nottingham and spent the afternoon at Uncle Parr's. Went with Aunt Alice to a bazaar with & then went a walk.

25th   Fine day. Father took the cart to Nottingham & I & Elizabeth Harvey came home. I have enjoyed myself very much.

26th   Fine day.

27th   Fine day. One of the steam engines of the railway came up with 10 carrages.

28th   Fine day.

29th   Fine day. Father went to Nottingham. Aunt Langford went to Ratclif (Ratcliffe) with Uncle & Aunt Robert. A steam engine and one carriage came to day and went to Derby, the first that had gone.

30th   Fine day. The line of railway from Nottingham. to Derby was opened but not for the publick till June 4th There were 4 engins; the 3 first had 6 carrages each and the last 2 – they looked very beautifull. Most of them had Union Gacks flying. There were several hundred people to see them pass.

31st   Fine day. Aunt Langford, E. Harvey & I went to Mr Barker's to tea & went to Clifton with Mr & Mrs Smith, Mr Kirkland, Miss Prowett, Mrs and Miss Mary & Fanny Barker. We enjoyed ourselves very much.

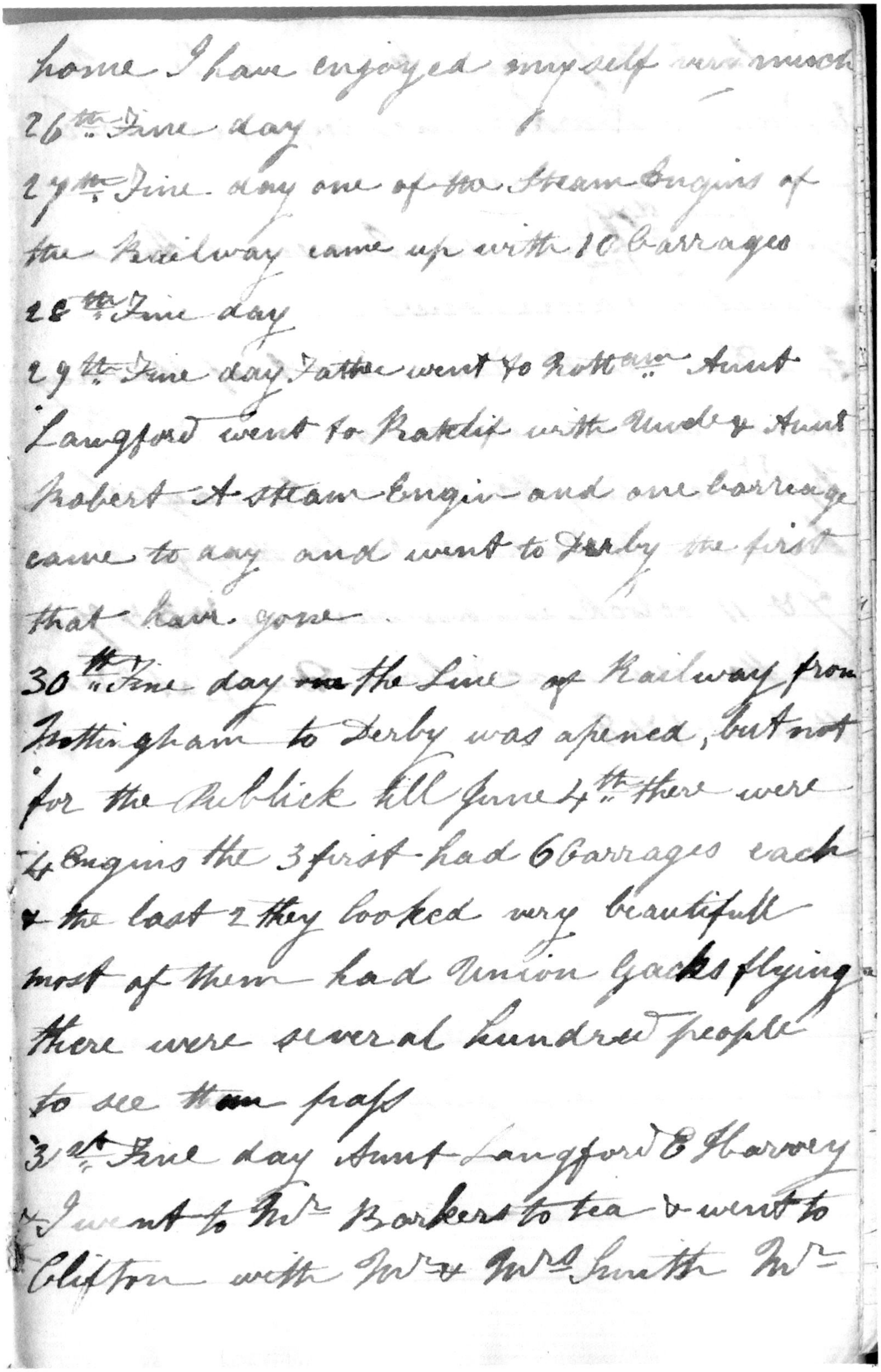

home I have enjoyed myself very much

26th Fine day

27th Fine day one of the Steam Engins of the Railway came up with 10 Carrages

28th Fine day

29th Fine day Father went to Nottm Aunt Langford went to Ratclif with Uncle & Aunt Robert A steam Engin and one Carriage came to day and went to Derby the first that have gone

30th Fine day the Line of Railway from Nottingham to Derby was opened, but not for the Publick till June 4th there were 4 Engins the 3 first had 6 Carrages each & the last 2 they looked very beautifull most of them had Union Jacks flying there were several hundred people to see them pass

31st Fine day Aunt Langford & Harvey & I went to Mr Barkers to tea & went to Clifton with Mr & Mrs Smith Mr

Fig. 9 Page of Elizabeth's diary highlighting the opening of the Midland Railway line in May 1839

Fig. 10 An early view of the Midland Counties Railway, Nottingham

June 1839

1st   Fine day.

2nd   Fine day. Cousin Ann Bailey came over.

3rd   Dull with rain most of the day. Fine in the evening.

4th   Fine day. The steam carriages have begun to rush to Derby. They go at 7 & 11 o'clock in the morning and 3 & 7 in the evening and leave Derby at 8 & 12, ½ past 4 & 8.

5th   Fine day. Mrs Harvey and Cousin Jane came.

6th   Fine day. Father and Aunt Betsy, Mrs Harvey, Cousin Jane & Elizabeth Harvey & I went in the cart to Derby to an Exhibition there (*which*) is in the Mechanics Institute Rooms. We were very much gratifyed with our visit.

7th   Little rain. 8th Fine day.

9th   Very fine day. We were very busy after tea. The railway trains brought a great many people from Nottingham. We could not find seats for them all. They took 12 carriages down from Derby. There were between 200-300 persons. The(*y*) could not take (*all*) who wated at the station till they came back about 4 o'clock at night.

10th   Stormy. Aunt Alice and Uncle John came in the evening by steam.

11th	Fine day. Father, Aunts Langford & Alice went to Derby in the cart.
12th	Fine day. Aunt Alice went home in the evening. I went with her by steam. I like the ride very much.
13th	Dull day. Came from Nottingham in the morning. Cousin Mary Nutt came last night.
14th	Rain most of the day.
15th	Fine day. Father & Aunt Langford went to Nottingham in the cart.
16th	Fine day. A good deal of company by railway in the evening. Several trains came up to Beeston Station extra.
17th	Fine day.
18th	Fine in the morning. A very grand Review of the Troops stationed at Nottingham on Bulwell Forist. Father took my Aunt Betsy and Alice, Cousin Mary & myself in the cart. There were a great many thousands of people. There we had a very good view of them. Just as they were concluding there came a most violent thunderstorm, and many hundreds had to regret the spoiling of their best bonets & dresses. We went to Aunt Fewkes to tea & had a pleasant ride home after the rain.
19th	Fine day. Miss Mary and Fanny Barker & Miss Prowett to tea.
20th	Fine day. Rain in the evening.
21st	Fine day. Cousin Mary Nutt went home.
22nd	Stormy. Father & Aunt Langford went to Nottingham and came home by steam.
23rd	Stormy in the morning. Fine in the afternoon. Very full of Company in the evening.
24th	Stormy.
25th	Fine day.
26th	Rain all day. Father and James Went to Nottm. for a Wagon load of timber to build a room in the garden.
27th	Showery. Began to build the room in the garden.
28th	Rain all last night and today. Father went to Nottingham by steam to see about some fireplaces for the new room.
29th	Dull day. Father and Aunt Langford went to Nottingham in the cart and brought 4 fireplaces and some ninepins.
30th	Fine day. I went to chaple in the morning.

July 1839

1st	Fine day. I saw Cousin Jane & Mr Moore in the railway.
2nd	Dull day. Five of the Miss Langfords from Lenton came to tea.
3rd	Fine day.
5th	Fine day. 7 or 8 to tea.
7th	Very fine and warm day. This is Beeston Feast. Mr and Mrs Ward, Uncle John & John came over. We had a very (*no entry*) deal of company by Railway.
8th	Fine day. A good deal of company bowling. There are 7 extra trains a day. The 3 first 3 days of the week. Eliza came over.
9th	Fine in the morning. Showery in the afternoon. Mr & Mrs Ward went home early this

morning.

10th   Fine day. Cousin Mary Nutt came in the afternoon. We walked to the railway in the evening with father and Mr Barker.

11th   Fine day.

12th   Fine day. Began to mow the meadow – had 5 men mowing.

13th   Fine warm day.

14th   Showery. I went to chaple in the morning.

15th   Fine day. had 3 men beside James and Father haymaking.

16th   Fine day. Had 20 men haymaking – got several loads from meadow – finished mowing.

17th   Dull day. Have got 27 loads of hay out of the Meadow – have 3 more to get.

18th   Rain all day.

19th   Rain some of the day.

20th   Showery.

21st   Fine day.

22nd   Rain part of the day. Mr & Mrs Harvey came over in the afternoon. A party came and brought there tea, etc. We found them water. There were 20 of them.

23rd   Showery. Mr Daykings party, 8 for tea.

24th   Showery, a very heavy storm of thunder and lightening about dinner time. A party of 42 to tea. They were Sunday School. teachers from the James Strutt Schools.

25th   Showery till 27th

28th   Showery. Cousin Mary and Miss Hopkin came over in the evening.

29th   Fine in the morning. Showery in afternoon. The Printers Party. 45 to dinner. There were a good many of them came by steam at 11 o-clock and went to play cricket in the meadow. Dinner was on the table at ½ 3 o'clock. They spent a merry day.

30th   Rain all day and all night very fast, indeed without intermission till morning.

31st   Rain all day. The Trent rising very fast.

August 1839

1st   Fine day. A large flood on the Trent.

2nd   Fine day. Got the hay in the Holme Close.

3rd   Fine day. Father went to Nottingham.

4th   Fine day. Aunt Langford & I went to chaple in the morning.

5th   Fine day.

6th   Fine day. Father went to Rudenton (Ruddington)

7th   Fine most of the day. Father and James went to Nottingham in the Pleasure Boat.

8th   Fine day.

9th   Fine day. Mr Jepson's . 25 to tea.

10th   Fine day. Rather dull. Father & Aunt Langford went to Nottingham.

11th   Stormy. I went to chaple in the morning.

12th   Dull day. Miss Blundall and friends came. This is the long-talked of 12 of Augst when the Chartists intend (beginning) their holaday.

16th	I went to Mrs Barker's to tea. Aunt Langford came after. Mr & Mrs Smith were there. Mr and Mrs Smedley are over from Adderbury (Attenborough).
17th	Miss Hannah Barker had this day gone to Liverpool to go to America with Mr J. Barker's 2 eldest children. Mrs Barker had gone to see them set sail. Mr & Mrs Smedley and I walked to the station house with them. They went by the 7 o'clock train to Biriming (Birmingham). It was a very sevear parting with all the family.
18th	Fine in the morning. Rain in the afternoon. Mr Cressey's & Bekat's fishing party. About 17 to dinner. They dined in the new room and then came into the house most of them. Went by the 9 o'clock train having spent a very merry afternoon.
22nd	Miss Hannah Barker sailed for America in the England sailing ship.

September 1839

10th	Fine day. About 10 to tea. Misses Barberrs, an accident on the railway above Chilwell. The 4 o'clock train went down at 7.
11th	Mr Morley's party. 8 to dinner. I went by the 4 o'clock train to Nottingham to stay a few days at Uncle Parrs.
22nd	Came home from Uncal Parr's. John came with me. We were too late for the train. Uncle Parr is going to leave Nottingham. The house they live in has been sold to be taken down. They are going to live at Ratcliff(e) on trent. I have been neglectfull indeed in not writing my diary. We have had a very wet Autumn. We have had very little dry weather for the last 3 months. Uncals Parr has gone to live at Ratcliff. Aunt Alice is gone with them.

November 1839

7th	Dull day. Father and Aunt Langford went in the cart to Ratcliff. Mr Barker's received a letter from Miss Hannah. She arrived in America safe and was much better (as well as little Henary) than she was when she started. They were 7[6] weeks making the voiage (voyage) and were very ill the first fortnight, being 3 weeks longer than they expected.
8th	Dull and damp all day.
9th	Dull day. Father & Aunt Langford went to Nottingham.
10th	Rain all day & most of last night. I have this day completed my 21st year.
11th	Very misty most of the day. Aunt Alice came over from Ratcliffe. We were very busy all day. Aunt Langford & I went to Beeston at night. Father went to Lenton Fair.
12th	Very misty all day. We have been keeping my birthday. We had Uncles John & Robert, Cousins George, Eliza & John Langford, Cousins Mrs Harvey, Jane & Mary Nutt. My Father, Aunt Langford, Aunts Betsy & Alice and myself had dinner in the dining room. Mr Harvey & Cousin Tom Nutt came after dinner. We gave all the women in the place a tea. Mrs Harwood & Mrs Nutt of Beeston, Mrs Wootton & Mrs Barker & all our own cousins had tea together in the large room. There were between 40 & 50 all together. My father engaged a fidler as soon as tea was over. We claired the tables away and dancing commenced. We gave the women a glass or two of wine each & when our own party were gone to supper they had ale & cake. (Uncle William came after tea). Dancing

was resumed & kept up till between 1 & 2 o'clock. Mr & Mrs Harvey & Tom Nutt went home. The rest of our cousins stayed all through the night & thus ended a day long to be remembered by all that were preasant and I think a merryer party never met before.

13th	Dull all day. My cousins all went home except Aunt Alice. Cousin Tom Nutt brought the cart for Jane & Mary.
14th	Very damp with rain nearly all day. Aunt Alice and I went to Mrs Writes (Wrights) and were caught in the rain.
15th	Dull and damp. Aunt Alice went home. Aunt Langford went to Nottingham with her.
16th	Finer day than we have had for a long time.
17th	Fine morning. Aunt Langford and I went to chaple. Rain in afternoon.
18th	Misty and damp. I went in the evening to call at Mrs Bradshaw at the other Public House. Mr Wilkinson left & gone to live at Nottingham.
19th	Fine with drying wind.
20th	Dull and cold. Father went to Nottingham.
21st	Dull with little rain. Cousin Tom Nutt came over in the evening and brought a bag for me to finish of Jane's.
22nd	Dull with little rain.
23rd	Fine day with drying wind. Aunt Langford & father went to Nottingham.
24th	Rain all day. Aunt Langford and I went to chaple in the morning.
25th	Very drying wind. Ann our servant went home to stay a few days.
26th	Fine day. Father went to dinner at Chillwell given to Mr T. Charlton, by (h)is friends.
27th	Cold and sharp frost.
28th	Cold. The ground covered with snow in the morning.
29th	Rain all day. James went home.
30th	Fine day. Ann came back. We have hired her again.

December 1839

1st	Fine day but very dirty. Aunt Langford & I went to chaple in the morning.
2nd	Very damp and misty.
3rd and 4th	Very damp and misty.
5th	Weather finer today.
6th	Very misty all day. Counsin Jane Nutt came. I walked some of the way home with her.
7th	Fine day. Father and Aunt Langford went to Nottingham.
8th	Cold and frosty. Aunt L & I went to chaple in the morning.
9th	Misty & Dull. I went to Lenton to spend a few days.
10th	Dull all day. Cousin Mary and I walked to Nottingham in the afternoon. Snow at night.
11th	Dull day. Mr and Mrs Godfrey and Mrs Harvey to tea and supper. We spent a very merry evening.
12th	Misty.
13th	Very damp with rain in the forenoon. Cousin Mary and I went to Mrs Harvey's to spend

the day. Mrs J. Harvey to tee. Mr J. Harvey, Cousins Tom Nutt & John Langford to supper.

14th   Misty and cold. Cousin Mary and I went to Nottingham in the afternoon.

15th   Mistey. Cousins Jane and Mary & I went to church in the morning. Mr Brown preached. Uncle and Nutt Harvey went; Mr T. Sharp to tea. Cousins Jane & Mary went to Mr Harvey's in the evening, and I came home. Cousin Tom came with me. We walked to Nottingham and from there we came by steam.

16th   Very mistey and damp. Aunt Langford is poorley.

17th   We have had a little sun to day, but still very mistey.

18th   Misty. We have killed a pig to day.

19th   Very damp. My Father went to Nottingham.

20th   Uncommonly damp. The wet runs down the walls in the Barr & Parlor. Very busy making poark pyis. A boy, grandson of Mr Hardy of Beeston got kicked very bad with a poney. My Father took him home in the light cart.

21st   Fine day. Father and Aunt Langford went to Nottingham. Sent a pye to Uncle Parr.

22nd   Dull with rain most of the day. Uncle John came by the 7 o'clock train.

23rd   Fine in the morning. Rain in the afternoon.

24th   Very rough wind. Father went to Nottingham. Mr Danvals & Marriott came.

25th   Very fine dry day. We have not had much company. Very little for Christmas Day.

26th   Fine most of the day. Rain at night. Uncle John came over in the afternoon.

27th   Frosty. Father went to Nottingham. A boy transported that my father caught on Tuseday for stealing some silk handkirchifs out of Mr Night's shop.

28th   Fine cold and frosty day. Eliza came from Clifton. She has left Mr Adams.

29th   Fine and frosty day. Aunt Langford and Eliza and I went to chaple in morning. John came over in the afternoon.

An account of bills paid for building the New Room in the garden.

To	Mr Roberts for bricks	£11 18s 0d
To	Mr. W. Surplice for Cant, etc.	1 0 10½
To	Mr H.M.Wood, for Coping, etc.	1 19 0
To	Mr J. Wilkinson, for Lime, etc.	2 0 0
To	Mr S. Pratt, Chimney Pieces, Hearths, etc.	3 15 0
To	Mr W. Liggett, for Nails.	1 2 11

(Cant bricks are a type of sloped brick)

An account of bills paid for building the new Rooms in the garden

	£ s d
to Mr Roberts for bricks	11 „ 18 „ 0
to Mr W Surplice for sand &c	1 „ 0 „ 10½
to Mr Wm Wood &c &c &c	1 „ 19 „ 0
Mr J Wilkinson &c lime &c	2 „ 0 „ 0
Mr S Bratt Chimney pieces hearths &c	3 „ 15 „ 0
Mr W Liggett for nails	1 „ 2 „ 11

Fig. 11 Account for the building of the 'New Room' at The Boat & Horses

Fig. 12 The 'New Room' as it stands today

January 1840

1st   Misty in the morning. Fine in afternoon.

2nd   Fine dry day. Cousin Eliza and I walked to Lenton. Cousin Tom Nutt has been very ill; is much better. Mary, William and George Cressey came part of the way home with us.

3rd   Fine and dry in the morning. Rain in the afternoon.

4th   Fine in forenoon. Rain in afternoon. Cousin Jane and Mr Moore came over to tea and went by the train. Father went to Nottingham.

5th   Very fine, frosty day. Aunt Langford, Eliza and I went to chapel in morning and evening Cousin Tom Nutt and Uncle John came.

6th   Fine, frosty day.

7th   Fine, frosty day. Canal frozen over in morning.

8th   Fine, frosty day. Aunt Langford and Eliza went to Nottingham.

9th   Frost in the morning. Thawing in afternoon. There have been six men taken up at Beeston supposed for breaking into Mr. Thornill's shop and stealing above £100 worth of wollen cloth.

10th   Sharp frost. Aunt Langford and Eliza went to Arnol (Arnold).

11th   Sharp frost. Father went to Nottingham.

12th   Sharp frost. Eliza went to Clifton.

13th   Drying wind.

14th   Dull in morning. Very fine afternoon. Mr Fox came to paint the doors etc. of the new room.

15th   Fine day, Cousin William Nutt and George Cressey came and brought a poark pye. Father went to Nottingham.

16th   Fine day. 17th Dull in the morning, fine in afternoon. Eliza came from Clifton.

18th   Rain most of the day.

19th   Stormy. Aunt Langford, Eliza and I went to chaple in the morning.

20th   Fine day.

21st   Very rough wind with storms of rain.

22nd   Rough wind etc.

23rd   Very rough wind.

24th   Very rough and stormy. I received a letter from Aunt Alice.

25th   Thunderstorm in the morning. Very large hailstones & snow fell at Beeston, Fine drying wind in the afternoon. Father, Aunt Langford and Eliza went to Nottingham.

26th   Stormy with rough wind. Aunt Langford and I went to chaple in the morning.

27th   Fine day. Aunt Langford and Eliza went to Nuttall (Nuthall).

28th   Rain in morning, fine in afternoon. Aunt Langford and I went to here Mr Hickling deliver a lecture on the art of printing and the printing press generally. He brought a press with him wich (which) was worked by some of there men. We were very much gratified. Came home in a most delightful storm of wind and rain.

29th/30th Showery. Flood on the Trent.

31st   Fine day. Mr Marriott of Gunthorp (Gunthorpe) came.

February 1840.

1st Stormy. Father, Aunt Langford went to Nottingham. Eliza went to Clifton.

2nd Stormy. Aunt Langford and I went to chapel in the morning. Cousin Tom Nutt came over at night.

3rd Fine in morning, rain in afternoon

4th Stormy.

5th Stormy. Trent rising fast.

6th Fine Day. Flood on the Trent. Aunt Langford and I went to here a lecture on electricity.

7th Stormy.

8th Stormy with hail in afternoon.

9th Fine with frost in morning.

10th Stormy. Victoria our Queen married this day to Prince Albert of Sax Coburg and Gotha in Germany. Great rejoicing in most of the towns in England, but nothing particular at Nottingham. Father went to dine at Nottingham.

11th/12th Fine day.

13th Fine day. I went to Lenton. Cousin Jane, Tom and Mr Harvey and I went to Batty's Circus at night.

14th Fine day. Cousin Jane, Mary & I went a walk in the afternoon.

15th Rain most of the day. Cousin Jane went to Hoveringham. Mary and I walked to Nottingham with her.

16th Fine warm day. I went to church in the morning with cousins. Came home at night. Cousin Tom walked home with me. Uncle John came by the train.

17th Stormy. I went to Beeston after tea.

18th Cold with very little snow.

19th Cold. Snow all day.

20th Cold with little snow.

21st Cold day, frost at night.

22nd Fine with very sharp frost. Father and Aunt Langford went to Nottingham.

23rd Very cold sharp frost. Aunt Langford and I went to chaple in the morning.

24th/27th Fine frosty weather.

28th Fine frosty day. Cousin Tom Nutt came at night. It is 16 years today since my Dear Mother died.

29th Fine with sharp frost. Father and Aunt Langford went to Nottingham.

March 1840

1st Sharp frost.

2nd Fine frosty day. George came over. Father went to Bradmore with Mr Cressey and Morley.

3rd Fine frost day. Shrove Tuesday. A party of Nottingham Gentlemen came in the afternoon.

4th Fine and frosty.

5th Very fine day. Busy gardening.

6th   Fine clear day. Gardening. Father making a path against the new room.

7th   Fine frosty day. Father and Aunt Langford went to Nottingham.

8th   Fine and frosty. Aunt Langford and I went to chaple in the morning. Uncle John came in afternoon.

9th   Fine day. Father went to the March fair. I went to Beeston after tea. Aunt Alice came by the 7 o'clock train. Cousin George walked over at night.

10th   Very fine day. Aunt Alice and I walked to Beeston in the morning to choose some flower roots at the Freckenings. I bought a Piras Japonacer. Aunt Alice went home after tea. Aunt Langford, Fanny Barker and I walked with her as far as Lenton. Cousin Eliza Langford went to live at Mr Wolley's at Beeston.

11th   Fine day. Received a letter from Cousin Mary Nutt.

12th   Fine day. 13th Fine drying day.

14th   Cloudy, drying day. Father and Aunt Langford went to Nottingham.

15th   Rain in morning. Fine in afternoon. Aunt Langford and I to chaple in morning. Uncle John and John Langford came at night. It is one year to day since my Dear Cousin Langford died.

16th   Cloudy day. Father went to a steeple chase run near Gamston.

17th/18th Fine cold day.

19th   Cold day. The Victoria Hotel at the railway opened by Mr John Stotard.

20th   Fine cold day.

21st   Cold day. Wind north by north-west. Father and Aunt Langford went to Nottingham

22nd   Very cold and cloudy. Aunt Langford and I went to chaple in the morning. Cousin Eliza came in the afternoon. Cousin Tom Nutt came at night.

23rd   Fine day. I went to the liberary at night.

24th   Fine day.

25th   Fine cold day, Cousin Mary Nutt came to spend a week with me. We went a walk in the evening.

26th   Cold day.

27th   Cold with rough wind. Aunt Langford, Cousin Mary and I went by the 3 o'clock train to (Long) Eaton to see the tunell at the Red Hill. We were highly gratfyed with our visit. They were putting up the Iron Bridge across the Trent. We walked home.

28th   Cold day. Cousin Mary and I walked to Nottingham. Came home by the train Father with us.

29th   Fine day. Cos Mary, Aunt Langford and I went to chaple in the morning. Tom Nutt came at night.

30th   Fine day. Cousin Mary and I went to the library in the evening. George came over at night.

31st   Cold day. Aunt Langford & Cos. Mary went to Nottingham. Mrs Cressey came back with them. Mary and I went to tea to Uncle Robert Nutt's.

April 1840

1st   Very fine day. Cos Mary and I took a walk by the Trentside in the afternoon.

2nd   Cold day. Mr Tom Godfrey came in the evening.

3rd   Very cold windy day. Cousin Mary and I walked in the evening.

4th   Fine day. Father and Aunt Langford went to Nottingham in the cart. Brought home a cannary bird and a passion flower plant Mr. Brown has given us.

5th   Fine day. Aunt Langford, Cousin Mary and I went to chaple in the morning. Mr & Mrs Harvey & Elizabeth came in the afternoon. Dear Cousin Mary went home at night.

6th   Stormy in the afternoon. I went to the liberry after tea. Cousin John Langford is out of his time to day at Mr. Oldknow's. He is 21 today.

7th   Cold & Stormy.

8th   Changeable.

9th   Fine day. Aunt Langford and I took a walke in the evening by the Trent side.

10th   Fine day. I went to Beeston after tea.

11th   Dull day with little rain at night. Father went to Nottingham

12th   Mild with rain, all day. Cousin Tom came at night.

13th   Fine day. I went to the liberry at night.

14th/16th   Fine day.

17th   Very fine day. Good Friday. Very busy in the afternoon. Cousin Jane, Mary & Tom, Mr Cressey, Mr Harvey and Mr Moore came. Father, Aunt Langford and I walked up the fields with them. Miss Baitman's party 14 to tea 9 others to tea.

18th   Fine day. Father went to Nottingham in cart.

19th   Fine day. Aunt Langford and I went to chaple in the morning. Cousin Eliza walked down. Cousin Tom Nutt and Cousin and Uncle John came. 5 to tea.

20th   Fine day. Mr James's party. About 26 to tea, 12 others to tea. Very busy.

21st   Cloudy. Mr and Mrs Harvey, Elizabeth and Nutt came in the afternoon. Father went to a steeple chase at Lenton. Mrs Tom Pailthorp died.

22nd   Fine day. Father went to fetch the Pleasure boat home. It has been repaired. 1 gent to tea.

23rd   Find day. They took Mrs Pailthorpe to Asson (?) to bury.

24th   Fine day. Mr Morley's party. 8 to tea.

25th   Fine day. Father and Aunt Langford went to Nottingham. in the cart. Cousin Mary Nutt came in the afternoon. I walked part way home with her. Jane came to meet her.

26th   Very fine warm day. Aunt Langford & I went to chaple in the morning. Cousin Tom Nutt went by the 7 o'clock train to Liverpool.

27th   Fine day. I went to the liberary in the evening.

28th   Fine day.

29th   Fine warm day. Aunt Langford and I took a walk in the evening.

30th   Fine day.

May 1840

1st   Fine and warm.

2nd   Fine and warm and very dusty. Father and I went to Nottingham in cart. I got out at Lenton. Cos. Mary walked with me. Cousins Jane and Mary came home with us. I walked to Beeston with them at night.

3rd   Fine warm day. Mr Cressey and Friends came. Cousin Eliza came down in afternoon.

4th   Fine day. I went to Beeston after tea. Cousins Jane and Mary came to. Aunt Hannah Jane received a letter from poor Tom yesterday. He has engaged to go to Sidney, New South Wales in the Anne Mary sailing ship.

5th   Fine day. The Railway opened to Leicester.

6th   Fine day. Father went to Nottingham.

7th   Fine in the morning. Stormy in afternoon.

8th   Dull and stormy. The partition put up in the large room. A young man named Hind killed at the railway below Beeston Station. He was collecting tickets after the train had started and sliped at the steps. The Leicester train being just behind passed over him taking off his head and one arm. They took him to the Victoria Hotel where an Inquest was held. 4 to tea.

Fig. 13 Beeston station in early Victorian times

9th	Rain all day. Father went to Nottingham.
10th	Rain all day.
	Rain nearly all the 11th/12th/13th
14th	Fine drying day.
15th	Stormy.
16th	Rain most of the day. Father and Aunt Langford went to Nottingham in the cart. Mr Fox finished painting the new room.
17th	Fine day. Mr Cressey and Harvey came over. Cousin Eliza and John came. 4 to tea.
18th	Cold and dull. I went to the library at night.
19th	Dull day.
20th	Drying dull day. 21st Fine day. 2 to tea.
22nd	Fine day. Finished whitewashing. Have had whole week at it.
23rd	Dull day. Father and Aunt Langford went to Nottingham in the cart.
24th	Stormy.
25th	Very rough drying wind. Blew a great many cherries off the trees.
26th	Cold stormy day. I went to Mr Barker's to tea.
27th	Fine day.
28th	Fine day. Mr Duffin went to Liverpool to see Cousin Tom Nutt.
29th	Fine day. I received a letter from my Cousin Tom Nutt.
30th	Fine day. Father (*and*) Aunt Langford went to Nottingham in the cart.
31st	Fine day. I went to chaple in the morning. 7 to tea.

June 1840

1st	Fine day. I Went to Beeston in the evening.
2nd	Stormy in the morning; fine in afternoon. I wrote to Cousin Tom. Miss Blundell & freinds by train. 13 to tea. Miss Poter (Potter) & friends.
3rd	(*no entry*)
4th	Very fine day.
5th	Fine day. Rain at night. Miss Blundell & Mrs Ireland came. Father went to Lenton. I went to Beeston, met Cousins Jane & Mary there.
6th	Fine day. Father & Aunt Langford went to Nottingham in the cart.
7th	Fine day. Whiten (Whitsun) Sunday. Mr Cressey came. Uncle Nutt went to Liverpool.
8th	Fine cold day. 9th Fine day. Very busy, several parties, 80 to tea altogather.
10th	Stormy in morning, fine in afternoon. 24 or 5 to tea. Father went to Lenton Fair. I have got a bad inflamation in one of my feet.
11th	Changeable.
12th	Stormy.
13th	Fine day. Father and Aunt Langford went to Nottingham in the cart.
14th	Fine day. Mr Cressey and children came by the train. Aunt Langford and I walked up the feilds with them.
15th	Fine day. Mr & Mrs Harvey came and brought Elizabeth to stay a few days.

16th   Fine day.

17th   Stormy. Mr Goodacre's party to tea, 74 of them. They came by train.

18th   Stormy. Went to Tea Meeting at Beeston held for the libary. 6 to tea.

19th   Stormy. 4 to tea.

20th   Fine day. Father and Aunt Langford went to Nottm.

21st   Fine in the morning, rain at night.

22nd   Stormy. Began to mow Mr Cartwrite's and Miss Bate.

23rd   (?) the other man's party. 28 to tea.

26th   Stormy. Mrs Harvey came to fetch Elizabeth Nutt with her. Mr Cressey went to Liverpool.

27th   Fine day. Aunt Langford went to Nottingham. Got one load of hay in the Holme Close.

28th   Fine day. Little rain in the morning, fine in afternoon.

29th   Fine day finished getting Home Close and the Garden Close.

30th   Stormy. Cousin Tom Nutt came home from Liverpool with Mr Cressey. He has persuaded Tom to return to his home rather than go to sea.

July 1840

1st   Stormy. Cousin Tom came in the evening.

2nd   (blank)

15th   Fine day. Aunt Alice came by the train and Mr & Mrs Weston with Mrs Nutt came to tea. They were over from Sleaford on a visit.

16th   Fine day. Mr Scals'es party. 57 to tea. 68 to Supper. Very stormy in the morning.

17th   Fine day. Mr and Mrs Weston, Mrs Nutt, & Aunt Langford went to the Exhibition.

18th   Fine day. Stormy at night. Father and Aunt Betsy & Alice and I went to Nottingham. Alice went home.

19th   Stormy.

20th   Fine in the morning. Stormy in afternoon. Cousin Tom came for me to go to Lenton. We went by the train.

21st   Fine day. Mary and I went a walk in the morning. Mr Moore came in the evening. He is over from Mancester (Manchester).

22nd   Fine cold day. Mr Cressy, Cousins Tom, Mary & I went to the Mechanick's Exhibition in the evening. We were highly gratifyed with our visit.

23rd   Fine day. Cousin Mary & I went to Nottingham in the afternoon to Mrs Harvey's to tea. Cousin Tom came up in the evening.

24th   Fine day. I came home. Cousin Tom walked with me.

25th   Fine day. Father went to Nottingham. Aunt Langford went to Ratcliff.

26th   Fine day. Rain in the afternoon. Cousin John came. 3 to tea. (Cousin Tom came in morning).

27th   Fine day.

28th   Fine day. A great cricket match played at Nottingham. Mr Harvey, Cousin Tom & Mrs Sharp came over in the evening.

29th   Fine day. Aunt Langford came home.
30th   Rain some of the day.
31st   Fine day. Cousin Tom came in evening.

August 1840
1st   Fine day. Father & Aunt Langford went to Nottingham.
2nd   Fine day. Four to tea.
3rd   Very warm day. I went with Cousin Jane, Mary and Tom to see Mr Frank Write's (Wright's) garden (*Lenton Hall*). It is a most pleasant place. 12 to tea.
4th/5th Fine & warm.
6th   Very warm day. Uncle & Aunt Nutt came to dine with us on peas and bacon. Aunt Langford went to see Cousin John. He is very ill but a little better than he has been. he has got a fever.
7th   Very warm day. Cousin Tom came in the evening.

Fig. 14 Lenton Hall, the residence of Francis Wright. Elizabeth described the Hall as 'a most pleasant place'.

8th	Very warm & dusty. Father & Aunt Langford went to Nottingham. Cousin John a very little better.

9th	Fine day. Cousin John a very little better. Cousins Eliza and Cousin Tom came.

10th	Fine day. Father, Cousin Tom & friends went to Wollanton (Wollaton) Hall and returned for tea. Miss Heath's party. 30 to tea.

11th	Stormy. Father went to Nottingham. Mrs Night came in the afternoon. She is over from London.

12th	Stormy.

13th	Fine day. Cousin Tom came for a bath in the morning. Aunt Langford went back with him to see John. He is a little better.

14th	Stormy.

15th	Rain in the morning; fine in afternoon. Father & Aunt Langford went in the cart to Nottingham I went by railway. Came in cart. (?) at exhibition.

16th	Dull day. Aunt Langford & I went to chapel in the evening. Cousin John came to stay a fiew days. He is a little better but recovers very slowly. Cousin Tom came at night and Mr. Harvey to tea.

17th	Rain in morning, fine in afternoon. Very rough wind & rain at night. Mr Wilds' party, 80 to tea and 82 to Supper. They brought their brass band with them.

18th	Fine in the morning, stormy in afternoon. 2 to Breakfast, 11 to tea. My poor Journal – I have quite neglected you for several weeks. The Nautilus chud (should) have been up. About 40 to tea. Mrs Cressey and friends with their children have been to tea, between 30 and 40 of them. They appeared to enjoy themselves very much.

Cousin Mary Nutt has spent a week with me. I have been to see Van Amburgh the Lion Tamer's performance at the Theater. I went with Cousins, Mrs Cressy, Mrs Harvey, Jane, Mary and Tom. We came to Lenton in the fly. I went to the Exhibition in the afternoon with Cousin Tom. Had tea at Mrs Cressey's.

October 1840

1st	Fine day.

2nd	Fine day. Father has gone to Nottingham Goose Fair. Cousin Eliza is come for a day or two. We walked to Clifton in the afternoon. Mr. E. Butler came home with us. Cousin Tom came at night. We walked to the railway.

3rd	Fine day. Father and Aunt Langford and Eliza went to Nottingham. Cousin George came home with them.

4th	Stormy. Eliza spent the day at Clifton and went home at night. Cousins Tom, Mary and Miss Sharp came in the evening. Went back by train.

5th	Dull day. I went by train to Nottingham. and met Cousin Mary and Miss Sharpe at Cressey's. I dined and had tea there. Came home by train. Cousin Tom, Mary & Miss Sharpe went to the Theater.

6th	Fine day. Cos Mary and Miss Sharpe came and spent the afternoon with me. They went by the train. I walked to the station with them. Aunt Langford has got a very bad cold.

Father went to Nottingham.

7th Fine day. The first day of the raises (races) at Nottingham. Father did not come home last night.

8th Fine day. Uncle John & a lady he calls my Aunt Mary came in the afternoon. Father arrived home by train at night.

9th Fine day. Very misty morning and night. I walked to Beeston in the evening and called at Mr Wolley's to see Eliza.

10th Fine day. Father and Aunt Langford went to Nottingham.

11th Very misty in the morning and at night. Aunt Langford and I went to chaple in the morning. Cousins Tom Nutt and John Langford came at night.

12th Very misty morning and night. I went to the liberary at night and had a very pleasant walk. Most beautiful and moonlight (moonlit).

13th Misty morning; fine day. Miss Ann Barker came home yesterday.

14th/16th Very dull weather.

17th Rain most of the day.

18th Stormy. Cousins Tom and John came in the evening. No other company at night. They walked home.

19th Rough wind. I went to the libery at night.

20th Dull day.

21st Dull and cold day. I went to Mrs Barker's in the evening. Miss Ann & Mary, Cousin Tom came over at night and fetched me home from Mr. Barker's.

22nd Dull day.

23rd Misty morning. Fine afterwards. Aunt Betsy cleaning parlour. She was taken with very bad pain in the back.

24th Fine day. Father and Aunt Langford went to Nottingham. Aunt Betsy no better; in bed all day. Aunt Langford went to Mr….

25th Fine day. Aunt Betsy about the same. I went to chapel in the morning. Cousin Tom Nutt came at night.

26th Dull day. Rain at night. Mr Hart gave the men that have potato ground of him a supper at our House. Aunt Betsy a very little better.

27th Fine in morning; stormy in afternoon. Aunt Betsy about the same. Aunt Langford went to Nottingham. for some medicine for her.

28th Dull day. Aunt Betsy very poorly. Mrses Dannels and Marriott came. James Rice died of smallpox – buried.

29th Rain most of the day. Aunt Betsy about the same. Sat up a little in the afternoon.

30th Fine morning, dull afternoon. Aunt Langford went to Nottingham for medicine. Mr… came to see Aunt Betsy. She appears about the same. She sat up in the afternoon a little. Misses Ann Mary & Fanny Barker called to see me in the afternoon. They are going back tomorrow to their places.

31st Very damp day. Father went to Nottingham.

November 1840

1st   Dull day. Father went to Newark. James took a horse to sell at the Fair tomorrow. Aunt Betsy a little better. Aunt Langford went to chapel at night. Cousins Eliza and John came. Eliza has had a very bad swelled face and been poorly, but is much better.

2nd   Rain in the morning; dark all day. Father arrived home at night. Was getting his Supper and accedently got a crumb in his windpipe, which made him very poorly. He sold the horse he to took to the Fair.

3rd   Damp with little rain. Aunt Betsy a little better. Aunt Langford went to Nottingham. The Misses Finns came in the afternoon. We killed a pig.

4th   Rain most of the day.

5th   Stormy. Cousin Tom Nutt and Josh Finn came at night. Been making the poark pyes.

6th   Stormy and very damp. Father went to Nottingham.

7th   Rain in the morning; fine in afternoon. Father and Aunt Langford went to Nottingham.

8th   Fine cold morning; rain in evening. I went to chaple in forenoon. Aunt Betsy came downstairs to dinner. I hope she will soon be well again. Cousin Tom came at night.

9th   Rain in morning; fine afternoon. I went to the library at night.

10th   Rain nearly all day. I have this day completed by twenty second year.

11th   Rain in morning; fine afterwards. Father went to Lenton Fair and bought a horse of Uncle Robert Harwood.

12th   Dull day. Cousins Jane and Mary came over in the afternoon. Cousin Tom came for them at night.

13th   Very damp with heavy rain all the afternoon. Father went to Nottingham.

14th   Flying showers. Father and Aunt Langford went to Nottingham.

15th   Fine cold day. Aunt Langford and I went to chaple in morning. Cousins Eliza and John came. A flood on the Trent.

16th   Rain in the morning. Fine with rough wind in afternoon.

17th   Fine morning, rain in afternoon. Uncle John Harwood was married this morning at St. Mary's Church, Nottingham to Mrs Mary Hanson, formyley (formerly) a Miss Nelson. They came by the ½ past 2 o'clock train. Two of Mrs. Harwood(s) brothers came. Father took them over the flood in the light cart.

18th   Dull day with rain at night. Uncle John with his Bride and her relations came by train and brought the wedding dinner to be cooked. Cousin Tom Nutt came to tea.

19th Nov to 5th Dec. Changeable.

December 1840

5th   Frosty morning. Aunt Langford and I walked to Nottingham. We got caught in a shower of rain at Lenton. We went into Uncle's until it was over. I saw Cousin Tom and Mary at Cressey's. Came home by train.

6th   Cold day. Cousin Tom and Mary Nutt came in afternoon. Aunt Langford, cousins Tom and Mary and I went to chaple at night. Mary stayed all night.

7th   Very cold day. Cousin Eliza is poorly. Aunt Langford went with her to a doctor at Nottingham. Cos Mary and I went by the train to Nottingham. Tom took us to see Mr

Puteros performance at the Theater.

8th   Rain all day. I spent the day at Lenton.

9th   Fine day. Cousin Tom walked home with me at night.

10th   Dull day. A gentleman here that is surveying Chilwell Burrows. Father went by the train in the evening to Nottingham.

11th   Dull day. Aunt L(*angford*) & I went to Beeston at night.

12th   Father and Aunt Langford went to Nottingham.

13th   Cold and frosty. I went to chaple in the morning. Cousin Tom came at night.

14th   Sharp frost. Father went to Nottingham by 2½ train.

15th   Fine frosty day. Father came from Nottingham.

16th   Snow in morning. Aunt Langford went to Ratcliff. Aunt Parr is very ill. Father came from Nottingham.

17th   Rain in morning. Fine afterwards. Aunt Langford came home

18th   Very cold & frosty. Aunt Langford & I went to Beeston at night. Eliza is better. We called to see her.

19th   Fine cold day. Father & Aunt went to Nottingham. William Brooks died of typhus fever.

20th   Dull and cold. Aunt and I went to chaple in morning.

21st   Very cold day. Nothing particular to write.

22nd   Very cold. Aunt Langford went to Ratcliff. I went to Beeston at night.

23rd   Sharp frost. Cousin Tom came in the afternoon. Father went to Nottingham.

24th   Sharp frost. Wm. Brooks buried in afternoon at Baptist Chaple. Aunt Langford came from Ratcliffe. Aunt Parr is a little better.

25th   Fine frosty day. Uncle and Aunt Jane came.

26th   Fine frosty day. Father went to Nottingham.

27th   Dull frosty day. I went to chaple in morning. Cousins John Langford & Tom Nutt came in the evening.

28th   Sharp frost. Cousin Tom came at night. I walked to Lenton with him to stay a short time.

29th   Sharp frost. Cousins Jane and Mary & I went to Nottingham. in the afternoon. Cos Tom went to the Glee Club at night.

30th   Sharp frost. Tom and Mary & I went to Mr Harvey's to tea. William came in the evening. Miss Coxon came from Dracott (Draycott). Rain at night.

31st   Cold day. Jane went to Miss Hudsons to spend the afternoon. Miss Hall came to dinner. She went back with Jane.

January 1841

1st   Thawing a little cousin May and I went to Nottingham to Mrs Birkets.

2nd   Fine cold day. I have nothing particular to write to day.

3rd   A very heavy storm of thunder, lightening, hail and snow early in the morning. Snow most of the day. I went to church in the morning. Sharp frost at night. Cousin Tom walked home with me.

4th   Sharp frost with snow nearly all day.

5th	Sharp frost with little snow.

5th   Sharp frost with little snow.

6th   Sharp frost, snow nearly all day. Father went to Nottingham.

7th   Very cold day. Canal frozen over.

8th   Very cold day. Aunt Langford and I went to Beeston at night.

9th   Sharp frost. Father went to Nottingham. Trent frozen over below Nottingham. Snow at night.

10th   Not quite so cold today. Snow nearly all the afternoon. Aunt Langford & I to chapel in morning. Cousin Tom came at night.

11th   Snow all day.

12th   Very cold with little snow

13th   Cold day. Father went to Nottingham. Cousin Tom scated up in the afternoon. William Harris taken up for robbing a boat.

14th   Cold day. I went to Lenton. Cousin Tom brought the cart to the station for me. Jane is very poorley with a sevear cold. Cousin Mary walked to Nottingham with me. Elizabeth Cressey came home with me to stay a short time. Tom came by train with us.

15th   Thawing all day.

16th   Continuous thawing. Canal broken up. Father went to Nottingham.

17th   Continuous thawing. Snow nearly gone. Cousin Tom came at night.

18th   Thawing. A very large flood when we arose this morning. We were quite surprised to see the water in the Croft. It is risen very fast.

19th   Fine cold day.

20th   Sharp frost. Father went to Nottingham. Aunt Langford went to Mr Thomson's for some medicine for Eliza. She is very poorley.

21st   Cold day. Cousin Tom came at night and made me a very hansome preasant of a scarf.

22nd   Cold day. I spent the evening at Mr Barker's.

23rd   Fine day. Father went to Nottingham. I went & met Cousin Mary at Mrs Cressey's.

24th   Fine and very cold. Aunt Langford and I went to chapel in morning. Cousins John & Eliza came in the afternoon. Eliza is a very little better.

25th   Fine, cold day. Aunt Langford and I went to the liberary at night. It is kept at Mr Wootton's now.

26th   Dull day. Mr Cressey came over to see his Elizabeth

27th   Fine, cold day. Gardening a little.

28th   Fine day.

29th   Clear, mild day. Gardening. Aunt Langford and I went to Beeston at night. Rain at night.

30th   Mistey with rain nearly all day. Father and Aunt Langford went to Nottingham.

31st   Dull with snow and rain in the afternoon. Cousin Tom came at night.

February 1841

1st   Sharp frost. Snow all day. Old Mrs Langford died aged 79 years.

2nd   Sharp frost. Snow nearly all day. Aunt Langford went to Clifton. George caled (called).

3rd   Snow all day.

4th   Very sharp frost. Received a letter from Aunt Alice.

5th	Very cold. Aunt Langford and I went to Beeston at night.
6th	Sharp frost. Father (*and*) Aunt L(*angford*) went to Nottingham. Cousin Eliza came. She is very poorly. Aunt put some leaches on her chest.
7th	Very cold. The snow is drifted to a great depth in some places. Aunt Langford went to Mrs Langford's funeral. She came home by train. Cousin Tom & George Cressy came in afternoon. Tom walked with me to Mr Wolley's in the evening. Eliza no better.
8th	Sharp frost. Cousin Tom came in afternoon for me to go to Lenton. We called to see Mrs Markam's Conservertary – it is the most splendid place I ever saw. Mr Moore has arrived to be married to Cousin Jane Nutt. He has been stoped (stopped) two or three days with the snow but has reached his lady love in safety at last. Very busy assis(*t*)ing to wrap up the wedding cake in the evening.
9th	Cousin Jane Nutt married to John Moore of Manchester at 9 o'clock this morning by the Rev'd C. Armstrong at Lenton Church. Uncle Nutt gave her away. Mary and I officiated as bridsmade's. Cousin Tom and Mr James Moore went to church with us. The breakfast party consisted of all my cousins Nutts, Aunt B. Nutt, Misses Finn and Hall, Mr Armstrong. My father came after breakfast. After drinking the health of the new married couple etc. Cos Tom, Mary, James Moore and I started of(*f*) with them to Castle Donnington in a carriage and pair of grays to Mr George Moore's w(*h*)ere we enjoyed ourselves very much. We arrived safe at home about half past 9 o'clock haveing left the happy pair to pass the honeymoon. We were received by a house full of company who were makeing merry on the happy occation.
10th	Cold day. Mr Sharp came in the afternoon.
11th	Thawing very fast, rain in afternoon. Expected Mrs Cressey. She did not come. We kept the wedding up with playing at bagertell etc., etc.
12th	Thawing and very dirty. Mr Sharp went home. Cos Mary and I walked to Nottingham with him and went to Mr Cressey's to tea. Cousin Tom and Mr Harvey walked home with us. Elizabeth Cressey went home.
13th	Dull with small rain nearly all day.
14th	Fine morning, rain in evening. Cousins Tom, Mary, Mrs Harvey and I went to church in morning and to Mr Harvey's to dinner and tea. We walked home to Lenton. I intended coming home but it rained so fast Uncle would not let me.
15th	Dull day, rain at night. Mr James Moore came in afternoon to pack <u>Mrs Moore's</u> boxes to send to Maccester (Manchester). Uncle received a letter from her yesterday; they got to Manchester on Friday night. My Cousin Tom brought me home after tea in the cart. I have spent a very happy week. Mr Beastall came and went home with Tom in cart.
16th	Dull day.
17th	Dull and misty with drisslin(*g*) rain.
18th	Frosty fine day. Our favourite dog Keeper died. We think he has been poisoned but how we do not know.
19th	Fine day. Father burried Keeper under a weeping ash on the grass plot. Aunt Langford

went to Nottingham with Eliza. She is very ill.

20th   Dull day.

21st   Fine day. Richard Nutt came in afternoon. Cousin Eliza came down in the evening. She is much worse – she went to bed as soon as she got here.

22nd   Fine day.

23rd   Fine day. Shrove Tuesday. Mr Thommson came to Eliza. He bled her. She is very ill. Today James went to Nottingham at night for medicine.

24th   Rain most of the day. Poor Eliza is about the same. She is very fainty at times.

25th   Fine day. Mr Thommson came in morning. Eliza Tho(r)pe is no worse to day.

26th   Flying showers. Aunt Langford went to Nottm. in morning. My Cousin appears a very little better today. I went to Beeston at night.

27th   Fine day. Father went to Nottingham. Dear Cousin about the same. Cousin George Langford, B. Butler and two Misses Voce's came to see Eliza. Mr Thommson came at night. Aunt Langford is poorley.

28th   Fine cold day. I went to chapel in morning. Eliza is about the same. Mrs Gretreck (*reports?*) that John Langford has been logging with came to tell us he is going to France. He went by the 11 o'clock train yesterday to London and was to get in Calice (Calais) today. He has gone without letting us know anything about it. Aunt Langford is very hurt aboutit to think he is so unkind. Cousin Tom came at night.

March 1841

1st   Dull with small rain all day. Cousin appears a little better this afternoon. I went to Beeston at night.

2nd   Dull with rain nearly all day. Eliza sat up all afternoon. She was not so well at night.

3rd   Fine day, rain towards night. Dear Eliza does not appear any better today.

4th   Dull, little rain towards night. Aunt Langford went to Nottingham for medicine. Cousin about the same. Received a letter from John. He arrived in France safe and well excepting a little sea sickness.

5th   Fine morning. Rain in the evening. Dear Eliza very ill. She (*h*)as a blister on her chest which is very painful.

6th   Fine day. Mr Thommson came. Eliza continues about the same. I went to Beeston in afternoon.

7th   Fine day. Dear Eliza much worse in afternoon. Rather easier towards night. The blister on her chest is kept open and is extremely painful. Cousin George came in afternoon, Cousin Tom at night. Received a letter from Aunt Alice. I sent one to post at night.

8th   Fine day. Father went to Nottingham. Poor Eliza a little better in afternoon, very ill at night. Mr and Mrs Langford came in afternoon. Aunt Langford went with then by train for medicine. Miss Ann Lees called in evening.

9th   Very fine day. Dear Eliza rather easier in morning, not so well in the afternoon.

10th   Misty morning. Very fine day. Eliza a little better.

11th/21st   Fine spring weather, warm with showers. Cousin Eliza continues better. I have nothing more particular to write.

21st   Dull day. Aunt Langford and I went to chapel in morning. Aunt sent a letter to John yesterday. Eliza holds better. Tom Nutt at night.

22nd   Stormy with rough wind. Father went to a steeple chase. I went to liberay.

23rd   Fine day. Cousin Mary Nutt came. Aunt Langford and I walked to the station with her. Eliza came downstairs.

24th   Fine dull day. I went a walk in evening.

25th   Fine morning, dull evening. I walked in evening.

26th   Fine and warm in forenoon, rain at night. Aunt Langford has got a very bad pain in her head. We went to Beeston at night.

27th   Fine day. Father, Aunt Langford and Eliza went to Nottingham. Aunt to Mr Ortons. Her head is very painful.

28th   Fine, growing day with slight showers. Eliza and I went to church in morning.

29th   Fine day. Rain in the evening. Miss F. Barker and I collected for the Bible Society. Went to the Library afterwards.

30th   Stormy with rough wind.

31st   Stormy and etc. Father went to Nottingham

April 1841

1st   Dull and cold with little rain at night. Eliza and I went a walk in the evening. Caled (called) at Mrs Barkers.

2nd   Fine day. Cousin Tom came in the evening. He and I walked to Beeston with Aunt Langford. We then went to a bazaar at Mr Bramleys.

3rd   Fine day. Father and Aunt Langford went to Nottingham. Aunt's head is very bad again. She went to Mr Ortons at night. Eliza (h)as a very bad cold.

4th   Fine dull day. Aunt Eliza and I went to chapel in the morning.

5th to 8th   Fine with growing showers.

9th   Dull morning. Fine afternoon. Good Friday. Busy day, 27 to tea. Cousin Tom at night.

10th   Fine day. Father went to Nottingham.

11th   Stormy. I went to chapel in morning. Walked with Cousin Tom in afternoon.

12th   Fine day. The Nautilus crew came up in the evening.

13th/14th   Stormy.

15th   Rain all day. Fine evening.

16th   Fine cold day. Father took Aunt Betsey to Ratcliff in the cart to stay a few days. Cousin Tom came in the evening.

17th   Fine day. Father, Aunt Langford & Eliza went to Nottingham.

18th   Stormy. Eliza went to Clifton. Cousin Tom came in afternoon. Mary Nutt and M. Sharp walked up in evening.

19th   Fine cold day. I went with Miss F. Barker to collect for the Bible Society. Went to Beeston afterwards. Cousin Tom at night.

20th   Fine day, rain in evening.

21st Stormy. Eliza came home. Father went to Nottingham.

22nd Stormy.

23rd Cold. Stormy morning, fine evening. Walked with Cos Tom at night.

24th Fine morning, stormy afternoon, rain all night. Father and Aunt Langford went to Nottingham. Father bought some wine. We have got a wine….

25th Stormy with rough wind. I went to chapel in morning.

26th Stormy morning. Fine with rough wind. Went to the liberrry in evening.

27th Very fine warm day. Mr Walter elected a member of parlament for the town of Nottingham. vacant by the death of Mr Ferguson. Mr Walter is a conservative and the first that has sat for the town of Nottingham for at least thirty years. He was opposed by a Mr Larpent wige (Whig) radical, but was elected with a ma (jority) of 238 votes.

28th Very fine day. Mr Walker was chaired. I suppose it was a most splendid sight. He was thought to be….

29th Fine day.

30th Fine day. Mrses Duffin and Hurstwites' party, 18 to tea. They came in pheatons and gigs. Cousin Tom came at night.

May 1841

1st Fine day. Father went to Nottingham. Aunt Langford has got an inflamation in her side. She went to Mr Orton's. Eliza went to Nottingham. Received a note from Alice.

2nd Stormy. Aunt's side continues about the same. She is very poorly. Mr Cressey came at night.

3rd Fine dull day. Eliza went to Derby to see for a situation but did not succeed in obtaneing one.

4th Rain in morning. Fine afternoon.

5th Stormy day with high wind. Aunt went to the Bible Committee at night. Cousin Tom came in the evening.

6th Rain in morning. Fine cloudy day.

7th Stormy.

8th Stormy. Eliza and I went to Derby by train. Eliza engaged to Lady Blains. My poor log. (I) have neglected you once more. Eliza went to Lady Blain's on the 13th May. Aunt Langford went to see her safe there.

30th Fine day. Whit Sunday. Cressey and Cousin Tom came.

31st Very fine warm day. Busy. 55 to tea.

June 1841

1st Fine day. 87 to tea. I went to Lenton. Cousin Tom brought a gig for me. We got to Lenton at ½ past 11 o'clock at night. We have been very busy.

2nd Fine and very dusty. My Father & Mrs Sharp, Cousin Tom & Mary and I went to a Conservative party at the Castel in honour of Mr Walter's election. There was a most magnificent display of blue. We enjoyed ourselves very much. There were between six and seven thousand persons there. A party of 44 to tea at home.

3rd	Fine, warm day. Mrs Cressey, Mr & Mrs Harvey, Mr Webster, the Misses Finn etc. have spent the day with us. My father came over in the morning having heard I was poorly (I was not well yesterday but am better). I walked in the afternoon with Cousin Tom for orders.
4th	Fine day. Mr Sharp went home in the forenoon. In the evening walked with Tom to the Trent Bridge's, and called at Cressey's.
5th	Stormy. Cousin Mary and I walked to the Trent in the evening.
6th	Fine, warm and dusty. I had a bad headac (headache) in the morning. In the afternoon walked with Tom to the cemetary and in the evening to the Trent.
7th	Cold and dull. Tom, Mary and I went to Nottingham after tea. A Chartist meeting in the Market Place.
8th	Rain in evening.
9th	Fine day. I came home. Cousin Tom brought me in a gig.
10th	Dull and cold. Received a letter from Cousin Eliza.
11th	Dull and cold. Cousin Tom came in the evening.
12th	Fine day. Father and Aunt Langford went to Nottm.
13th	Find day. Aunt Langford and I went to Chapel in morning. Cousin Tom came in afternoon. I have a very bad cold.
14th	Fine, very cold for June. Cousin George Langford came in afternoon, Cousin Tom in evening. I walked to the Libery.
15th	Fine day. 16th Fine day. Father went to Nottingham.
17th	Fine. Thunder at a distance. Have mown the Home Close on Wedensday and got it today.
18th	Day of June was celebrated at our house by a party of gentlemen haveing dinner. About 30 of them. Mr Cressey in the Chair. A very heavy thunderstorm when we were setting dinner on table.
19th	Rain most of the Day. Father went to Nottingham.
20th	Stormy day. Cousin Tom came in evening. I wrote to Mrs Moore.
21st	Fine day. Miss Mary Barker went with me to the liberry.
22nd	Fine with showers at a distance.
23rd	Fine day. Thunder at a distance. We got 13 loads of hay out of the Meadow.
24th	Thunder storms. Father let the men go with mowing the meadow.
25th	Rain nearly all day.

——-*No more recorded for 1841*——-

January 1842

1st	Mild day and very dirty. I am spending a few days at Lenton. Cousin Mary, Miss Coxon and I went to Nottingham in afternoon. Called to see Mrs Cressey. She has got a little daughter. It was born on Thursday morning.
2nd	Fine cold day. I went to Church in morning. Cousin Tom walked home with me in afternoon. I received a letter from Aunt Alice.

3rd	Cold. I went with Miss F. Barker to collect for the Bible Soci(e)ty in the afternoon.
4th	Frosty day. Nothing particular to write.
5th	Cold day.
6th	Cold day. I went to the libarry. Mr W. Wootton is very ill.
7th	Fine day. Frost at night.
8th	Sharp frost. Father and Aunt Langford went to Nottingham.
9th	Sharp frost with small snow at intervals all day.
10th	Sharp frost. I went with Miss Fanny Barker to collect. We afterwards walked down the Trent side.
11th	Sharp frost with little snow at night.
12th	Cold day. Several gentlemen of the Nautilus crew came up. Went back by train.
13th	Cold with snow all day.
14th	Snow nearly all day. Father finished getting the trees out of the fields that have been takein down.
15th	Sharp frost. Father went to Nottingham.
16th	Sharp frost in the morning with rain all day. Snow melting very fast. Cousin Tom came in afternoon. I spent a very comfortable evening with him.
17th	Thawing in the morning; frost in evening.
18th	Cold with rime and mist. 4 to tea.
19th	Sharp frost and very misty. Busy makeing poark pyes.
20th	Sharp frost. I sent a pye to Lenton.
21st	Very cold day.
22nd	Thawing in morning. Excessively cold with wind, rain and snow. Father and Aunt Langford went to Nottingham
23rd	Sharp frost. The roads very slipery. Aunt Langford and I went to chapel in morning. Elizabeth Cressey came in afternoon with Mr Duffin and friends in a featon (phaeton)
24th	Very cold day. Went with Miss Barker to collect. Walked by Trent side afterwards. Elizabeth C. with us.
25th	Snow in morning.
26th	Thawing with high wind and rain at night. Cousin Tom came in evening.
27th	Thawing very fast.
28th	Fine cold day with slight showers of rain. A very large flood water came on very fast in the Croft.
29th	Frost in morning. The water risin(g) much in the night. It came down the Croft as far as the little window in the taproom. Father went to Nottingham. Uncle John took him over the water in the light cart.
30th	Sharp frost. Water going down.

February 1842

4th	Cold day. A stoppage at the lock caused by the lock bursting.
5th	Fine cold day. Father and Aunt Langford went to Nottingham.

6th   Cold day. Aunt Langford, Elizabeth Cressey and I went to Chapel in morning. Cousin Tom and Mr Cressey came in evening.

7th   Cold and very dirty. E. Cressey and I went to Beeston in afternoon.

8th   Damp day. Mrs Hustwaite & friends to tea. Ball at Cresseys. The Glee Club.

9th   Fine day. The stoppage at the lock over, a great many boats here. Cousin Tom, Mr Cressey, G. Webster, etc. came in afternoon. All tired out with their last night's ball.

Fig. 15 The lock keeper's house at Beeston Rylands

10th   Very fine warm day. Working in garden in afternoon.

11th   Stormy day.

12th   Fine with very rough wind. Father went to Nottingham. E. Cressey and I walked to Beeston.

13th   Stormy with rough wind. Aunt Langford and I went to chapel in morning. Cousin Tom came in evening and took Elizabeth Cressey home. Mr Cross of Beeston died very sudenly today. He was teaching the Sunday School scolars at the Baptist Chapel. He was reading the 55 Chapter of Is(*iah*), a chapter he had been requested to read to the children by a boy that had been in the school and is now gone to be a sailor. He had read nearly through the Chapter when he fell backwards and died in about three hours. A letter from Alice.

14th	Fine day. Went in afternoon with Miss Fanny Barker.
15th	Very fine day. Father bought a horse of Thomas Ratcliff
16th	Misty morning, fine afternoon. Father went to Nottingham. Aunt Langford busy dressing beds.
17th	Fine day.
18th	Fine day. Cousin Tom & Mr Cressey & G. Webster came.
19th	Fine day. Father and Aunt Langford went to Nottingham.
20th	Misty morning; fine but overcast. Aunt Langford went by train to Nottingham to walk to Ratcliff.
To 25th	Stormy. Aunt Langford came home.
26th	Fine morning. Stormy afternoon. Father and I went to Nottingham. I met Aunt Alice there. Went to Castle Lodge to tea.
27th	Stormy. Cousin Tom came in afternoon.
28th etc.	High winds.

March 1842

6th	Fine day. Aunt Langford and I went to chapel in morning. Cousin Tom in after. 2 to tea.
7th	Stormy day. I fell down the celler steps. Hurt myself but not seriously.
8th	Fine day, stormy evening. George Milton cutting the apple trees, made me a strawberry bed. William Shipman came.
9th	Stormy. Aunt Langford finished dressing beds.
10th	Fine day. The Judge came into Nottingham. Frank Wright, esq. is the Sheriff. He was attended by about 300 gentlemen on horseback. Cousin Tom was amongst them. He afterwards went to church. Mr Brown preached. T(om) came up in evening; we walked to Beeston.
11th	Fine morning, stormy afternoon.
12th	Fine day. Cousin Tom came to bring a calf father has bought.
13th	Fine morning, dull afternoon. Aunt Langford and I went to chapel in morning. Two to tea, Mr Curfet(?) and Smith
14th	Fine day. Busy making poark pyes. I went to liberry in the evening.
15th	Dull day. A letter from Eliza. She is very ill.
16th	Overcast. Father went to Nottingham.
17th	Fine morning, Dull afternoon. Rain at night. Mrs Stenson and Mrs Berrington called.
18th	Stormy. I walked to Beeston at night.
19th	Fine morning, rain in afternoon. Father and Aunt Langford went to Nottingham. Mr J. Wild and friends in afternoon.
20th	Stormy.
21st	Stormy, Father went to Ratcliff.
22nd to 24th	Generaly fine mornings and rain in afternoon & night.
25th	Fine morning, overcast. Good Friday. Very busy, 11 to tea. Mr Cressey and Cousin Tom came.

26th   Stormy. Father and Aunt Langford went to Nottingham.

27th   Dull day. I went to Chapel in morning. Cousin Tom came in afternoon. 2 to tea.

28th   Fine morning, dull afternoon. Mr Alliott's party, 13 to dinner, 6 to tea. Two young men of the names of Taylor and Lowater drownded out of a pleasure boat at Wilford. Young Alliott's father and two uncles, Mr Wild and docter Attenborough came having heard it was Master Alliott that was drowned.

29th   Fine day. The Nautilus crew came up. 24 to tea and coffee.

30th   Fine morning, rain in afternoon. Father went to Nottingham.

31st   Stormy with rain all night.

April 1842

1st   Stormy. William Wootton's little boy died last night, aged 7 years.

2nd   Very cold day. Flood in Trent. Father & Aunt Langford went to Nottingham. Took our measures to be marked. Poor William Wootten, father of the little boy above, died of consumption, aged 33 yrs.

3rd   Fine, overcast at times. Aunt Langford and I went to chapel.

4th   Fine day. Miss M. Barker and I walked to Beeston in evening.

5th/6th Fine days. 5 to tea.

7th   Fine day. W. Wootton & son buryed. Aunt Langford went to funeral.

8th and 9th Fine days and very cold night.

10th   Fine cold day. Cousin Tom came in afternoon. We walked by Tren tside.

11th   Cold and overcast. Miss Barker and I walked to Beeston in the evening.

12th   Cold and dull.

13th   Very cold day. Father and I went to Nottingham. Met Aunt Alice their (there).

14th   Rain most of the day.

15th   Fine day. I went to Beeston at night.

16th   Fine and cold. Father & Aunt Langford went to Nottingham.

17th   Cold and overcast. I went with Miss Barker to church in morning. Received a note from Aunt Alice. Aunt Parr something better.

18th   Fine day. Walked with Miss M. Barker to Beeston in evening.

19th to 24th Fine warm days, and frosty night.

24th   Fine day. I went to chaple in morning. Cousin Tom came in afternoon, Aunt Betsy has got a very bad finger. Aunt Langford and myself had colds. 4 to tea.

25th   Very warm and dusty. Mr and Mrs Finn, Mrs Sharp came to tea. I went to Beeston in evening.

26th to 29th Warm dry days, frosty nights.

30th   Fine day.

May 1842

1st   Fine day. Went to chapel in morning. Mr & Mrs Hopkin to dinner. Cousin Tom in afternoon, 4 Frenchmen to tea.

2nd   Find day. Mr Morley & Thomas Hopkin to dinner. Misses M. & F. Barker and I went to

Beeston in the evening.

3rd   Dull day, rain in evening. Mr & Mrs Langford and family to tea. Aunt Langford very bad cold. Aunt Betsy's finger something better.

4th   Fine cold day. Father to Nottingham.

5th   Dull day with rain at night. Miss M. Barker and I went to hear a Mr Burns lecture who is a New Zealand cheif. His face is tattooed all over very beautifully. He was a cheif eight years. He gave us a description of their manners, customs, their religions, their amusements, manner of going to war, etc. etc. He was dressed in a cheiftans costume. He had several war clubs etc. with him. I was very much amused.

6th   Dull with slight showers. Father and I went to hear Mr Burns conclude his lecture. Mrs Burns played on the music glasses with which I was very much pleased.

7th   Very heavy showers all day. Father and Aunt Langford went to Nottingham. Cousin George came by train with Aunt. He stayed all night.

8 th   Stormy. 8 to tea.

9th to 14th Generally fine.

15th   Fine day. Whit Sunday. Cousin Tom came over in afternoon & William.

16th   Fine day. Very busy day.

17th   Very warm day. Busy with company, 84 to tea.

18th   Fine day. 14 to tea. 134 Sunday School children came to tea. They brought their things with them. Aunt Langford went to Nottingham in morning. Father went to Lenton. William brought the cart for me. I went in afternoon.

19th   Stormy. Betsy Watts, Mrs Hannah Nutt and children, Cousin Tom went to dinner to Mr Hicklin, Mises Edowers and Finn to supper.

20th   Rain at times dureing the day. Mrs Cressey and Mrs Thorp walked down in the evening. Cousin Mary and I went to Nottingham and bought some worstard (worsted) to work two waistcoats.

21st   Fine day.

22nd   Fine day. C. Cressey, William and I went to church in morning. Aunt Nutt and Mr Cressey went to London by railway. Tom went to Nottingham and took Aunt's things. Mr Moore came last night. He and Mr James Moore came to tea. Tom and I walked to the Trent Bridge in the eveing. Got caught in rain. Called at Mrs Richard's and Mrs Handley's.

23rd   Fine day. Walked with Tom in evening. Mr Moore went home.

24th   Rain in morning.

25th and 26th Fine day.

27th   Fine day. Aunt came home. She has enjoyed herself very much.

28th   Very warm day. I came home. Cousin Mary walked with me.

29th   Fine day, 4 to tea.

30th   Fine day.

31st   Very warm. Aunts Langford and Betsy went to Ratcliff to see Aunt Parr and Aunt Lockton. They are both very ill. 8 to tea. The Nautilus crew up. Cos Tom at night.

June 1842

1st to 4th Fine weather.

5th   Fine day. Cousin Tom came in afternoon.

6th/7th   Fine.

8th   Fine day. Aunt Betsy went to Ratcliff. Aunt Langford went to Nottingham with her. Cousin Mary came in afternoon and went by train to Dracote (Draycott). Mr Folds has opened 2 singing classes at Beeston. I have joined them, paid 10s 0d for the course of lessons. This is the first night. Went with Miss Mary, Fanny & Jane Barker.

9th/10th   Fine warm weather.

11th   Fine day. Father went to Nottingham. I went to my lesson in evening.

12th   Very warm day.

13th   Warm with little rain in afternoon.

14th   Fine day. Cousin Tom came at night. Mr Canning staid all night. 17 to tea.

15th   Fine day. Third lesson in singing.

16th   Fine, dull at night. Very busy whitewashing. We got (up) at ½ past 3 in morning., am very tired.

17th   Fine day. 6 to tea.

18th   Dull with rain in evening. Father and Aunt Langford went to Nottingham. Singin(g) in evening.

19th   Fine, growing showers. 1 to tea.

28th   Fine day. Began to mow.

29th   Fine day. Aunt Betsey came home. Aunt Fowkes came for a few days.

July 1842

1st   Rain in morning. Fine afterwards. The Printer's party. 30 to dinner and tea.

2nd   Stormy day. Aunt Fowkes went home.

3rd   Fine day. Cousin Tom came in afternoon. We walked down to the meadow.

6th/7th   Fine day. Finished getting in the hay. Had 38 loads out of the meadow.

10th   Fine day. Beeston Feast. 8 to tea. Uncle and Aunt John, Mr & Mrs Ward Cousin Tom came in evening. He is keeping house a(t) Mr Cressey's.

14th   Fine day. I went in the evening to Clifton with Mr Smedley, Mr J Cross, Misses Ann, Mary and Fanny Barker. Cousin Tom came in evening.

19th   Rain most of the day. The Nautilus party. 17 to dinner, 20 of the Band to dinner. 110 to tea. They had a marque(e) in the meadow. Tea at twice in the large room. Very merry party; went home by the ½ past 10 o'clock train.

21st   Fine day. The Nautilus came up at night.

23rd   Fine day. 4 to breakfast.

24th   Very hot day. Aunt Langford and I went to church in afternoon. Met Cousin Tom in the feilds. He went to church with us. The Nautilus came in the evening. 21 of them to tea and coffee.

26th   Very fine day. Father went to London. An inquest over a young man that was drowned in the Trent whilst bathing held at Bradshaws.

27th   Fine day. 31 to tea. Mrs Langford came.

28th   Fine day. Rain at night. Mrs Langford came. 17 to tea. Miss Davenson's party. The Nautilus at night; had beans and bacon to supper. Began to mow oats. A very good crop.

29th   Fine day.

30th   Fine day. Aunt Langford & I went to Nottingham.

31st   Fine day. George Langford spent the day with us. To chaple in morning.

August 1842

1st   Fine day. Father came home from London haveing enjoyed himself very much. Cousin Tom came at night.

2nd   Very warm day. Cousin Tom and I went to Derby by the 11 o'clock train and returned by the 8 o'clock.

3rd   Fine day. 9 to tea. I went to my singing lesson in the evening.

4th   Fine day.

5th   Fine day. Mr Walter elected a(n) M.P. for Nottingham.

6th   Rain in morning. Fine afternoon. I went to my lesson at night.

7th   Fine day. I went to church in morning. Aunt Langford went to Clifton at evening. Mr Cressey came. 7 to tea.

8th   Fine day. Mr Herbert's party – 42 to tea. A special train to Matlock. I am very tired tonight.

9th   Very fine day. Mr Fred Lee's party. 2 to tea.

10th   Fine morning, rain evening. Mr Stegman's party. 72 to tea.

11th   Fine day. I walked to Beeston in evening. Mr Spencer and party.

12th   Fine day. Cousin Tom came in evening. He and I walked to the station to meet father. Went to Nottingham yesterday and came home by the 9 o'clock train tonight.

13th   Very warm day. I went to Nottingham.

14th   Exeptionely warm. I went to chapel in morning. 8 to tea.

15th   Very warm. Went with Miss Fanny in the afternoon.

16th   Dull day. 5 to tea.

17th   Fine day. I went to my singing lesson at night.

18th   Fine day.

19th   Find day – rain at night. Aunt Langford went to Beeston at night.

20th   Fine day. I walked to Chilwell in evening. Singing lesson afternoon.

21st   Rain nearly all day. Tom came in afternoon.

22nd   Fine day.

23rd   Fine day.

24th   Dull with rain in evening. Went to my singing lesson.

25th   Rain nearly all day. Father went to Nottingham. The Nautilus came up in evening.

26th   Dull morning, fine afternoon. Father and I went to party at the Castle.

27th   Dull day. I went to the lesson at night.

Fig. 16 The 'party' at Nottingham Castle. It celebrated the election of John Walter as member of parliament for Nottingham

28th   Fine day. I went to chapel in the morning.
29th   Dull morning, fine afternoon. Aunt Langford went to a tea party at Bethal Chapel.
30th   Fine morning, rain afternoon. A letter from Eliza. She is very ill. Also one from John. He is enjoying very good health
31st   Fine day. Went a walk by Trent side in evening with Miss Mary Barker. 2 to tea.

September 1842

1st   Dull day.
2nd   Very fine day. Mr Duffin and friends in afternoon. The Nautilus in evening. Mr Court etc. 16 to tea and coffee.
3rd   Fine day. Father & Aunt went to Nottingham.
4th   Fine day. Uncle and Aunt John came to dinner. Cousin Tom came in afternoon. We walked by the Trent side.
5th   Fine day. I went by train and then by coach to Ratcliff and found Aunt Parr very poorly.
6th   Fine day. I walked up to the mill in forenoon.
7th   Fine day. Aunt Alice went to Nottingham.
8th   Fain. Aunt Alice very bad head.
9th   Dull day. Aunt Alice went in the evening to collect for the Missionary Society.
10th   Stormy. Aunt Alice and I went and looked over the Mill in afternoon. We got weighed. Aunt was 7½ stone and I, 8 stones 10 lb.
11th   Fine day. Aunt Alice and I went to church in morning and afternoon. Mr Berry preached a most beautiful discourse in the afternoon. We walked down to Aunt Laxtons(?) in evening. She is very ill.
12th   Fine day. I expected Cousin Tom would fetch me home. He did not come. Aunt Parr did not get up to day.
13th   Fine day. I went a walk with Mrs Harries in evening.
14th   Fine day. Came home by the carrier to Nottingham and then by train. I called at Mrs Langford's. Went to my singing in evening with Miss Mary & Fanny Barker.
15th/16th Though dull, Cousin Tom came in afternoon.
17th   I went to my lesson at night.
18th   Fine day. Cousin Tom came in afternoon. He (h)as been very ill. (H)as had the colery (cholic) very bad. Tom glad to see he is something better.
19th/20/21st Changeable.
21st   Singing at night.
to the 25th Generaly fine. I went to church in morning.
26th to 30th Changeable. Nothing particulary to write.

October 1842

1st   Fine day. Father and Aunt Langford went to Nottingham. I went to my singing lesson in evening.
2nd   Very fine day. Went to church in morning. Cousin Tom came in afternoon. We walked by the Trent side.

3rd	Fine day. Father went to Nottingham.

3rd   Fine day. Father went to Nottingham.

4th   Fine day. Father staid all night last night at the Fair.

5th   Fine day. I went to the Fair in afternoon. Miss Sharp and Cousin Mary, then Cousin Tom made me a preasant of a very han(d)some work box. I came home by the ½ past 7 train.

6th   Fine cold day. Father went to the raices. Aunt Langford and I went to Clifton in afternoon. Lady Bruce, daughter of Sir Juckes Clifton. She is married to Sir Henry Harvey Bruce. It is their first visit since being married. They were in a carriage with four beautiful gray horses. They were met by the Farmers on horseback and with the Band playing. The men had dinner and horsemen had tea. George put us over in Sir Jucke's boat.

7th   Fine day. Father went to the raices.

8th   Dull day. Aunt Langford went to Nottingham. I went to my lesson in evening.

9th   Dull day, 4 to tea.

10th   Fine day. Went with Miss Fanny and Mrs Trigg in afternoon. A - collecting to (for?) the liberry in evening.

11th   Fine day. Father met with a sad accident. He was riding a young mare and with coming down Meadow Lane she threw him. Some men that were at work in a field saw it and went to his assistance. One of them brought him home. He was not consious of what had happened to him for more than half an hour after he got home. We were very frightened. We did not know what to do to him. We sent for Mr Orton and told him to go to bed and keep very still. He went to bed but got up again in the afternoon. He had a good deal of fever towards night.

12th   Fine cold day. Father much better this morning. Miss Mary Barker and I went to Lenton to see the new church consecrated (by) the Bishop of Lincoln. Delivered a most eloquent and appropriate sermon from Haggai (?)2nd, 9v. The glory of this latter house shall be greater than of the former saieth the Lord of Hosts; and in this place will I give peace saith the Lord of Hosts. The church was full. I was most pleased with the service. The collection amounted to £175. We went to Uncle Nutt's to dinner and tea, and went to our singing at night.

13th   Fine and cold.

15th   Fine and cold. Father went to Nottingham.

16th   Fine cold day. I went to Nottingham in morning. Cousin Tom came in the afternoon. Went to Nottingham. 5 to tea.

Fig. 17 Lenton Parish Church. Elizabeth attended the newly consecrated church on 12 October 1842

17th   Dull day. Aunt Langford went to meeting at Nottingham.

18th   Dull day.

19th   Very cold day. Aunt Langford went to Ratcliff. Father to Nottingham. I went to my singing at night. We had a very grand night of it. There was a good deal of company that and I thought we sang very well.

20th   Very sharp frost in morning.

21st   Sharp frost. Aunt Langford came home. Aunt Parr is very ill. She is much worse.

22nd   Very stormy. Father was taking with a bad ague fit in the night. Aunt Langford and I got up and made him some tea and a fire in his bedroom which did him good.

23rd   Dull and cold. I went to chapel in the morning.

24th   Cold day. Went to liberry in evening.

25th   Dull day.

26th   Stormy. I went to my singing lesson in evening.

27th/28th   Dull and stormy.

29th   Cold day. Father and I went to Nottingham. Cousin Eliza came home from Worth Rectory, near Ripon. She has left her place partly through ill health, poor dear girl. Finished my singing. I am very sorry indeed.

30th   Fine day. I went to church in morning. Cousin Tom came in afternoon, 3 to tea.

31st   Cold day.

November 1842

1st   Very fine day. Aunt Langford and Eliza went to Nottingham. Cousin Mary Nutt came in afternoon. Cos. Tom in evening.

2nd   Dull day. Father went to Nottingham

3rd   Fine cold day. Eliza and I walked to Beeston in afternoon.

4th   Cold and stormy. Aunt Langford and I went to Beeston at night.

5th   Stormy. Father and Aunt Langford went to Nottingham. Eliza went to Ratcliff.

6th   Fine day.   Sunday at home all day. 3 to tea.

7th   Very dull and damp. I went to Beeston in afternoon.

8th   Rain nearly allday.

9th   Rain all day.

10th   Dull day. I have this day completed my twenty fourth year. How very quickly the years fly.

11th   Fine in forenoon, rain in afternoon, and night. Father went to Lenton Fair. Mr John Sharp's Uncle died last night. Young Bonser's horse ran away with him and threw him against Mr Pick's yardgate and cut his face very severely.

12th   Stormy morning. Fine afternoon. Father and Aunt Langford to Nottingham.

13th   Very wet day. Cousin Tom came in afternoon. He gave me pencil case, very nice one. We sent Mrs Harvey a bottle of cream.

14th   Dull day. Aunt Langford and I went to Lenton in afternoon to see about a girl, Heard that Miss Kirkland was taken to the Assilam (asylum) last Friday. Poor thing, it is a very bad job.

15th   Dull day, rain at night.

16th   Stormy day.

17th   Dull and damp. Cousin Tom came at night. Mr David Finn and Mr William Surplis have parted this week.

18th   Fine cold day. Gardening. Mr Duffin came in afternoon.

19th   Very stormy and damp. Father went to Nottingham. Eliza came from Ratcliff. She is very poorly. Aunt Parr is no better.

20th   Fine morning, dull afternoon. Aunt Langford and I went to chapel in morning. 3 to tea.

21st   Dull day. Eliza very poorly.

22nd/23rd Little snow.

24th   Fine day. Eliza is a little better. Our servant Elizabeth (Ruston or Preston) left. She has been 4 years with us. We engaged Eliza Pass in afternoon.

25th   Fine day.

26th   Dull day.

27th   Damp day. Rain at night. Cousin Tom came in afternoon.

28th/30th   Very dull and damp.

December 1842

1st   Very damp and dirty. Our new maid came.

2nd   Damp day.

3rd   Damp day. Father and Aunt Langford went to Nottingham.

4th   Fine morning; dull day. Eliza went to Clifton yesterday. Cousin Tom came in afternoon.

5th   Damp day. Miss Barker came in afternoon.

6th   Dull day.

7th   Very misty. Richard Mills brought a pig.

8th   Fine day

9th   Dull day

11th   Damp and misty. Father, Aunt Langford and I went to Nottingham. Aunt went to Ratcliff. Aunt Parr is very much worse. Cloudy and damp. Cousin Tom came in afternoon. He told me his Father has taken a house in (*no entry*).

12th   Fine day.

13th to 16th   Dull day. Very fine, warm nights.

17th   Fine drying day. Frost at night.

18th   Fine day. Eliza came from Clifton yesterday. I went to church in morning. 5 to tea.

19th   Dull day. Mr Elleott and Mr Wild. 2 to tea.

20th   Fine warm weather.

21st   Fine morning. Rain in afternoon. Aunt Langford came home by the 11 o'clock train and went back by the 2 o'clock. Aunt Parr a little better. Uncle's cows all ill. Their servant has left them.

22/23rd Very mild weather.

24th   Cold day. Father and I went to Nottingham. Father lost a basket coming home with a goose and a pound of tobacco in it.

25th   Sunday. Christmas Day. Very sharp frost in morning.

Written on separate slip of paper.loose, at back of volume

'Better a little with the fear of the Lord, than great
treasure and trouble therewith'.

Poem on Last Page

Of all the fools on earth by heaven accursed,
The druncerd shuld be reconed with the worst.
No Beast that walks the plane or bird that flies
Lives not so base a part and so uncivil (*ised*)
The dull, the slow, the poor, dispised ass
In wisdom does the drunkard far surpass.
It drinks no more when nature satisfied
But leaves the stream along the vail (vale) to glide
But drunkards of inferior sense will drink
Till they can neither walk, nor talk, nor think.
What sin will not the drunkard then commit
Whilst in this vile intoxacated fit
Satin can rule him then with easy sway.
And turn him as he pleases in his way.
His health, his wealth, his caricter and (mind?)
Are all distroied by this atrocious crime
We censure him

67